the informal economy

Making It In **Rural America**

ELAINE L. EDGCOMB

TAMRA THETFORD

FEBRUARY 2004

FIELD
(Microenterprise Fund for Innovation,
Effectiveness, Learning and Dissemination)
The Aspen Institute
One Dupont Circle, NW, Suite 700
Washington, DC 20036
(202) 736-1071
www.fieldus.org

Acknowledgments

There are many people to thank for their assistance in completing this study. First and foremost, continued thanks go to Jack Litzenberg, Senior Program Officer for the Charles Stewart Mott Foundation, who first called attention to the size and significance of the informal economy in the United States, and to those in that economy who make their living through entrepreneurial activities. Jack generated the questions that have guided this work and all the components of the informal economy research project, and has pushed us to learn how enterprise development services might be better designed to serve their needs and support their business success.

Sincerest thanks go to those in western Nebraska who closely helped us with our research, but who will remain anonymous to preserve the confidentiality of the entrepreneurs we interviewed. They include our recruiter, who introduced the project to her contacts, encouraging individuals to speak with us, organizing the interviews, and managing many other administrative aspects associated with the research. Without her on the ground assistance, this research would not have been possible. Our hosts at the courthouses, libraries and churches that served as interview sites all provided gracious hospitality and facilities for conducting the interview sessions.

Our gratitude also goes to Rose Jaspersen at the Nebraska Microenterprise Partnership Fund for her interest in and support of the research. Other individuals who provided context and comments included: Gene Severens, National Fund for Enterprise Development; Joan Hanson, GROW Nebraska; Barry Dunn, South Dakota State University; Arlis Moore, University of Nebraska Food Processing Center; and Jon Bailey, Center for Rural Affairs.

We remain grateful for the collaboration we have had with the staff of the Institute for Social and Economic Development on implementing the whole informal economy research project, and particularly the exchange and support of Jan Losby. We have benefited greatly from their experiences in doing this same research in other communities.

We acknowledge the support of our communications team at Aspen, including Carol Rugg for her comments and guidance in the creation of this document, Colleen Cunningham and Greg Landrigan for their help in the production of the text, and Jackie Orwick for managing the electronic dissemination of all information on the informal economy research project.

Finally, we extend our sincerest appreciation to the 42 individuals who participated in interviews and shared their experiences with us. While the text focuses principally on the 29 with the lowest income in the group, all of them contributed to our understanding of economic life on the Great Plains today. How can one not be struck by the sheer determination and hard work that these individuals exhibit as they struggle to "make it" on a land and in communities they hold dear? One cannot help but walk away impressed from hearing these stories of people who generally try to play by the rules, and yet who feel that they have to bend them a bit to keep their families together and their dream of a rural life alive.

Elaine L. Edgcomb
Tamra Thetford

Table of Contents

Executive Summary

This study summarizes and reflects on the experiences and perceptions of 42 low-income individuals who work informally in western, rural Nebraska, and most directly focuses on the experiences of 29 of them who are low income. The work is financed by the Charles Stewart Mott Foundation, a sustained funder and observer of microenterprise initiatives in this country, and is part of a broad inquiry into the place of microenterprise in the U.S. informal economy. Overall, the research is designed to answer the following questions:

- What is the nature and scale of the informal economy in the United States?
- How do microenterprises operate within the informal economy?
- What are the implications for practice? Could informal entrepreneurs be potential clients for microenterprise services? And, if so, what would be required to help them grow their businesses?
- What are the implications for policy? Are there specific governmental policies and/or regulations that might be changed to facilitate informal entrepreneurs' growth and ultimate movement toward the formal economy?

Complementing this study is a literature review prepared by staff of the Institute for Social and Economic Development (ISED) and the Aspen Institute's FIELD program, and two studies of Latino and African American participation in the informal economy, the first prepared by FIELD and the second prepared by ISED.

For the purpose of this study, the informal economy is defined as that component of the overall market in which enterprises, employers and self-employed individuals engage in legal but unregulated activities. While they do not comply with standard business practices, taxation regulations and/or other business reporting requirements, they are otherwise not engaged in overtly criminal activity. It includes both employed and self-employed workers; cash is the most common medium of exchange; and inferior work conditions are commonplace for workers.

Interviews were conducted with informal entrepreneurs in seven counties of western Nebraska. Ranch country, the region is characterized by small and declining populations, great and widespread poverty, and persistent downward trends in earnings and rural income. This has pushed many in the area to depend on entrepreneurial activities to fill the income gap. Ranch households constituted 45 percent of the low-income sample. The remaining 55 percent were townspeople. The sample contains interviews with seven males (24 percent) and 22 females (76 percent). Forty-five percent of the group is between 31 and 45 years old, while another 41 percent is between 41 and 60. All of the interviewees are white. Seventy-nine percent of the sample had at least a high school education. Fourteen percent reported annual household incomes below $20,000. Fifty-two percent had annual incomes between $20,000 and $30,000. The remaining 21 percent had incomes above $30,000. Most interviewees were married. Only three were single, divorced or separated.

The respondents were actively involved in patching income from a wide range of small-scale income generating activities alongside either ranch work or primary wage jobs. In all, the 29 respondents engaged in 51 formal and 39 informal activities, an average of 2.75 economic activities per respondent. Only one informal business was conducted on a full-time basis. On average, the annual earnings reported for each informal activity were $4,061 (median $3,250), and the informal activities represented 17 percent of household income (the median was 13 percent). Business assets were quite low, as well. The average value of reported assets was $3,364 (median $900).

In most cases, the informal economic activities were very small-scale, low revenue-generating operations. Oftentimes, these activities were "layered" one on top of another, each fitting in a way that efficiently uses up available "downtime." The informal activities in almost every case were designed to be a portion of individual and household income, and even when interest was expressed in growing the business, only a few were interested in it becoming full time. Additional revenue was the goal, but for ranch households, the ranch remained the primary concern. In addition, for both ranch households and non-ranch households, the need for benefits and a constant stream of income lead people to value and hold onto formal employment when they can get it.

There are four motivations that underlie the multi-tasking and dependence on informal work that is a normal part of the work life of these respondents and their spouses. They include: risk mitigation — reducing their vulnerability to the vagaries of ranching; the lack of other good employment opportunities; the small-scale returns of each endeavor, leading them to add on more; and, in some instances, a reluctance to grow due to either fear of the management challenges or the press of child care and other family commitments. Informal entrepreneurs justify the informal nature of the activities in several ways. They see them less as businesses and more as just another way one works to make a little money. The activities are considered so small-scale or erratic that they're not considered worth reporting. In some cases, the activity is new and being tested to see if going formal is worth it. And, in some other instances, the activity is engaged in as part of a bartering arrangement. The exchanges are rarely explicitly quantified or recorded.

The respondents' informal activities could be classified into three groups. A small number were engaged in informal work in which they offered their labor for hire or for agreed-upon products and other services. The largest group was engaged in self-employment or microenterprise activities designed to provide supplementary revenue to their households. These activities were in the areas of arts and crafts, foods, services and animal-related industries. Finally, there were a small number of "growth potential" businesses in which the owners demonstrated an interest in expanding the businesses and possibly formalizing them. These individuals were more attuned to the market, manifested strong skills and an entrepreneurial spirit, and lived in households where conditions either supported, or demanded, the ratcheting up of the business.

The entrepreneurs in the study approach the issue of formalization in a variety of ways and can be placed in a hierarchy according to their level of compliance with (or interest in complying with) the requirements of legal registration, adherence to regulations and taxation policies. The majority of the group (72 percent) operated at least one business in a totally informal manner. Twenty-eight percent of the group operated at least one business in which they followed some "rules of the game." Three entrepreneurs (10 percent) have a formally recognized business on which they declare part of their income, but pocket some amounts for household or personal use. One entrepreneur (3 percent) was ready to take all the steps necessary to formalize her business, and there were eight others who had taken varying steps to explore the idea (31 percent of the group), but none was ready to take the leap. Trying to make a good calculation of what would be lost and what gained through formalization was hard for them.

While this research suggests that a third or so of all informal entrepreneurs would be candidates for assistance from microenterprise services, programs would need both to increase their marketing and adapt their services to reach this group. This group could benefit from the type of sound business analysis and guidance that is embedded in high-quality microenterprise programs, especially if these services could be adapted to the specific needs, and time and place constraints of these busy entrepreneurs. This involves increased marketing (most of the entrepreneurs in this group had never heard of any microenterprise services) and tailoring marketing messages so that those who don't describe their activities as businesses will still see themselves as targets for the services on offer. But, it's more than just changing the message; it's also changing the products or services on offer. These entrepreneurs could benefit from feasibility assessment focused on the pros and cons of growing a business and taking it formal, coupled with "risk mitigation" planning for helping those interested in making the transition. Step-by-step descriptions of the formalization processes for specific types of businesses may speak to those who want to know concretely what is involved up-front before committing to the time and energy involved in the process. They would also be responsive to information and strategies to reduce their costs and increase their markets. As important as the content are the delivery vehicles. These entrepreneurs generally express resistance to any long-term training process. In addition to short courses, distance learning and extension-style technical assistance models may allow microenterprise programs to leverage their work with far-flung rural entrepreneurs.

Delivering these services, however, demands resources. Nebraska already has a number of strong microenterprise support organizations, but their resource levels are stretched very thin, especially for providing support to rural areas. With only 13 staff from seven organizations serving a broad area, it is not surprising that there are many entrepreneurs who haven't heard of their services. And, while the state of Nebraska has been a supporter of microenterprise development for some time, channeling funds through the Nebraska Microenterprise Partnership Fund for re-lending and re-granting to microenterprise organizations across the state, the question is whether current levels of investment are sufficient to reach informal entrepreneurs like these. This study suggests that many of the tools and strategies required to reach informal entrepreneurs can be built upon the services already provided. What's required now is to expand and deepen these efforts for the benefit of many more.

Introduction

This study presents a look at rural Nebraskans operating in the informal economy. As part of an ongoing research effort aimed at better understanding informal work in the United States and its implications for both policy and practice, this study summarizes and reflects on the experiences and perceptions of 29 informal business people who live and work in seven rural counties in western Nebraska.

The work is financed by the Charles Stewart Mott Foundation, a sustained funder and observer of microenterprise initiatives in this country. While the U.S. field has grown enormously over the last 15 years, both in numbers of programs and numbers of individuals served, there still remains a large gap between the estimated size of the market and the documented reach of microenterprise program services. The *2002 Directory of U.S. Microenterprise Programs*,[1] for example, lists 650 programs located in all 50 states, the District of Colombia, the Mariana Islands and Puerto Rico, of which 554 provide loans, training or technical assistance directly to microentrepreneurs. The approximately 300 organizations that provided detailed data reported serving 100,000 individuals in 2000. Based on estimates of the likely reach of those programs on which detailed data could not be obtained directly, the field may actually have reached between 150,000 and 170,000 individuals that year.[2]

At the same time, research has documented the presence of much greater numbers of low- to moderate-income microentrepreneurs, many of whom practitioners believe are hampered in their efforts to build strong businesses by a lack of capital, technical assistance, training, networks and other resources commonly available to other businesses. ACCION USA-commissioned research, for example, has estimated 13.1 million microentrepreneurs in the U.S. (defined as either someone who is self-employed or a business owner with five or fewer employees), of whom 10.8 million have never received a bank loan for their businesses.[3] Estimates made by Aspen Institute staff, drawing on U.S. Department of Commerce survey data and other sources, indicate as many as 2.3 million of these entrepreneurs are low income.[4] These research findings have led the Mott

[1]Britton A. Walker and Amy Kays Blair, *2002 Directory of U.S. Microenterprise Programs* (Washington, D.C.: The Aspen Institute/FIELD, 2002).

[2]The estimates use MicroTest data as a proxy. MicroTest is FIELD's performance data collection project that annually aggregates and analyzes data from programs across the U.S. (53 in 2001; 73 in 2002). The lower estimate is based on using the median number of clients (205) served by these programs in FY 2000; the higher number is based on the median number of participants (273) for these same programs. Participants are defined as any individuals receiving any level of service from a program during a given year; clients are those who receive more substantial services: a loan or more than 10 hours of training, technical assistance or other services during the fiscal year.

[3]ACCION USA, *Executive Summary: The Microlending Market in the U.S.* (October, 1999).

[4]Peggy Clark and Amy Kays, *Microenterprise and the Poor* (Washington, D.C.: The Aspen Institute, 1999), 77. Low income is defined as having household income below 150 percent of Department of Health and Human Services poverty line. For a family of four, that threshold was $17,417.

Foundation to question whether the gap is due to not only a lack of resources or a lack of institutional capacity, but also to a mis-match between the services offered by microenterprise programs and the needs and circumstances of many of these entrepreneurs. Hypothesizing that a large portion of them may operate in the informal economy and under assumptions distinct from those of many program operators, the Foundation has initiated a broad inquiry into the subject, of which this study is a part. Overall, the research is designed to answer the following questions:

- What is the nature and scale of the informal economy in the United States?
- How do microenterprises operate within the informal economy?
- What are the implications for practice? Could informal entrepreneurs be potential clients for microenterprise services? And, if so, what would be required to help them grow their businesses?
- What are the implications for policy? Are there specific governmental policies and/or regulations that might be changed to facilitate informal entrepreneurs' growth and ultimate movement toward the formal economy?

To answer these questions, the Foundation has commissioned both FIELD at the Aspen Institute and the Institute for Social and Economic Development to undertake a number of research activities. These include:

- The completion of a literature review on the informal economy in the United States;
- A review of current microenterprise program practice with respect to informal entrepreneurs;
- Qualitative research with informal entrepreneurs in several settings;
- A convening of researchers and practitioners to explore the findings; and
- The development of summary findings and recommendations for both policy and practice.

Documents related to the first two tasks have been released and are available on the FIELD Web site.[5] In addition, a set of studies examines the experience of informal entrepreneurs and workers in distinct communities. The first two of these studies document informal economic activity in African American and Latino communities, the first by the Institute for Social and Economic Development and the second by FIELD. These are also available on the FIELD Web site.[6] This report is the third in the series and looks at informal activity in rural communities. Subsequent documents will summarize overall research findings and recommendations.

---

[5]Jan Losby and others, *Informal Economy Literature Review* (Washington, D.C.: The Aspen Institute/FIELD, December 2002); available from http://www.fieldus.org/li/pdf/InformalEconomy.pdf; Internet; Erika Malm, "The Informal Economy and Microenterprise in the United States," *FIELD forum* Issue 14 (Washington, D.C.: The Aspen Institute/FIELD, March 2003); available from http://www.fieldus.org/publications/Field_Forum14.pdf; Internet.

[6]Jan Losby and others, *The Informal Economy: Experiences of African Americans* (Washington, D.C.: The Aspen Institute/FIELD, September 2003); available from http://www.fieldus.org/publications/IE_AfrAm.pdf; Internet; Elaine L. Edgcomb and Maria Medrano Armington, *The Informal Economy: Latino Enterprises at the Margins* (Washington, D.C.: The Aspen Institute/FIELD, September 2003); available from http://www.fieldus.org/publications/IE_Latino.pdf; Internet.

What Is the Informal Economy?

To place the findings in this report in context, it is helpful to have at least an initial understanding of the informal economy in the United States.[7] And, the first thing that must be understood is that it is quite large. Microfinance practitioners engaged in international development have long understood how pervasive informal work is overseas. Informalization of work arrangements is a powerful global economic force that affects billions of people, especially in poor countries. While its presence is overwhelmingly obvious in the mega cities of Africa or South Asia where millions of people, caught in vicious circles of poverty and powerlessness, struggle to survive, hawking single cigarettes, cheap watches or small food items, many Americans are not used to thinking about the informal economy in the U.S. Yet, clearly many millions of people in this country lead economically "informal" lives: the Guatemalan "houseguest" who swaps household chores for room and board; the guy who's always on the corner selling sweaters and hats in winter, tee-shirts and shorts in summer; the handyman who offers you a better price for a new kitchen cabinet if you pay in cash.

The estimates of the size of this economy vary from researcher to researcher, but the impression that all these estimates convey is that the informal component of the U.S. economy, while not matching that of developing nations, is surprisingly large and possibly growing. Economists have measured it as a percentage of GNP, and estimated it to represent between 4.4 percent and 27 percent of that sum, with most estimates centering on 10 percent. The current GNP figure equals $10,678 billion. Therefore, the value produced in the informal economy is $1,067 billion annually, using the 10 percent figure. In other words, for every $10 produced, $1 comes from the informal economy.[8] Other researchers have estimated it to include up to one-seventh of the economically active population of the country, using firm size as a proxy. Still others have noted that it includes substantial numbers of workers in certain occupations (close to 84 percent of all child-care workers and 20 percent of all seamstresses, for example), and in certain localities. (Twenty-nine percent of the Los Angeles County population, which includes large numbers of immigrants, has been estimated to work informally.)[9]

But, what is the informal economy? For the purposes of this research, it is that portion of the economy identified by the following four characteristics:

- It is *legal but unregulated:* Enterprises, employers and self-employed individuals do not comply with standard business practices, taxation regulations and/or other business reporting requirements, but they are otherwise not engaged in overtly criminal activity. As presented here, the informal economy should not be confused with the underground economy, which may include trade in drugs, prostitution and other illicit commodities.

---

[7]Losby and others.

[8]U.S. Department of Commerce Bureau of Economic Analysis, National Income and Product Account Tables (July 8, 2003); available from http://www.bea.doc.gov/bea/dn/nipaweb/TableViewFixed.asp?SelectedTable=17&FirstYear=2002&LastYear=2003&Freq=Qtr; Internet.

[9]Losby and others, 32-35.

- It includes both *employed and self-employed workers,* with some engaged in both kinds of work. Individuals may hire themselves out irregularly or may be steadily employed at factories operating "under the radar." Or, they may be operating full- or part-time businesses, which are either totally or partially generating revenues without a paper trail.
- *Cash is the most common medium of exchange,* although bartering also occurs. This enables participants to hide income from taxation. Workers and microentrepreneurs don't claim it on income tax forms, and employers don't file employment records.
- *Work conditions for those who labor are inferior* to those found in the formal economy. Earnings, security and environmental protections are less. Equipment may be out of code or unsafe, and there is no protection from exploitation.[10]

Women and men, the poor and non-poor, immigrants, the educated and the less educated all engage in the informal economy. They do so for a variety of reasons. For some it is an economic necessity, their only resort or a better alternative to other low-wage formal employment available. Others are involved in informal work for personal fulfillment, social obligation or as a means of supplementing their primary income. The majority of informal economy participants are employees, working for others, in sweatshops or out of their homes in contract relationships to producers. But, many are also self-employed. The very nature of being a micro — or very small — enterprise lends itself to operating in the informal economy. These enterprises are largely invisible or operate at low levels of visibility. They may or may not have licenses, and are often engaged in casual hiring, non-reporting of income and other informal labor practices. They can be easily moved, opened or closed at will, and thus, can hide from regulation.[11]

Finally, it is important to note that the formal and informal economies are connected. Participants may combine earnings from informal self-employment with wages from formal employment, or transfer payments, such as public benefits, or investment income or savings. Or, they may be employed both formally and informally at the same time (a factory worker who also works for cash, part time, in a cleaning business). They engage in these activities to generate additional income in low-wage markets and to create an economic buffer to cover periods of unemployment. Informal work arrangements may also be a strategy imposed from the outside as big firms restructure and outsource functions to subcontractors both to minimize costs and maximize flexibility. Under these arrangements, they push workers out of the formal economy into the informal economy where they suffer without protections of the legal system. Workers are found who move fluidly back and forth between the two worlds, some by necessity, and others by choice.[12]

---

[10]Losby and others, 5-8.

[11]Manuel Castells and Alejandro Portes, "World Underneath: The Origins, Dynamics, and Effects of the Informal Economy," *The Informal Economy: Studies in Advanced and Less Developed Countries,* eds. Alejandro Portes, Manuel Castells and Lauren A. Benton (Baltimore: Johns Hopkins Press, 1989), 11-37.

[12]Losby and others, 11-12.

What This Study Is About

This study examines the place of rural entrepreneurs within this context. Its intent is to understand:

1. What is the nature of informal economic activities within rural communities?
2. Why do people participate in the informal economy? What incentives exist for informal economic activities and what barriers hinder participation in the mainstream economy?
3. What are the survival strategies of rural residents who participate in the informal economy? How are informal economic activities patched together, with each other and with more traditional income streams, to support individuals and their families?
4. How do informal microentrepreneurs not participating in microenterprise development programs differ from those who have approached programs for services? Are there differences in business size or the revenues generated?
5. What are the opportunities for and barriers to growth for informal enterprises?
6. What are the implications for microenterprise development programs?

To answer these questions, qualitative, open-ended interviews were conducted with 29 low-income individuals in seven rural counties in western Nebraska. The results of these interviews are reported in the pages that follow. Chapter 2 describes the respondents and the communities in which they live and work. Chapter 3 describes the overall characteristics of the informal work that these respondents engage in. Chapter 4 offers a closer look at the enterprises and work activities of low-income respondents, their motivations and attitudes toward formality, and considers the future prospects of these activities. Chapter 5 reports the expressed needs of informal entrepreneurs for services, and discusses their perceptions on formalization. Chapter 6 presents recommendations for both policy and practice. Finally, Appendix A presents the research methodology used.

A Quick Look at the Respondents and Their Context

They live on ranches and in small towns in western Nebraska. They are ranchers, horse trainers, day laborers and makers of ranch gear. They are quilters, crafters, bread and jelly makers, photographers, lawn mowers, housecleaners and day-care providers. All these jobs and more are done informally in Nebraska's rural counties by ranch families and townspeople aspiring to sustain their families and remain in the communities they love. Consummate jugglers of multiple jobs, they patch their livelihoods together in complex ways. While the informal work or enterprise may be a small part of the whole, it is often the piece that fills a "dead" season, that pays essential bills or provides the extra income that raises a household above the survival level. This section will present the context in which these informal activities are found, and profile the individuals who engage in them.

The Context

Western Nebraska is ranch country. Dominated by the cattle industry, the counties[13] in which this research took place are lands of extraordinary beauty full of the wide open spaces, great skies and rolling landscape that are hallmarks of the West to many Americans. In contrast to the splendor of the external environment, the economic and social landscape presents a picture of hardship and challenge. The smallest rural counties there, and the sites of this research, are characterized by a set of features that inform this picture:[14]

- *Small in size and declining in population:* These counties are small in population, with no population center of 2,500 or more. They sit in the Great Plains region (an area including the agricultural and ranch areas of Nebraska, Kansas, Minnesota, North and South Dakota) that has lost nearly 9 percent of its population from 1990 to 2000, a loss largely due to the flight of young adults seeking work in metropolitan areas once schooling is completed. The result is that "over 40 percent of the population [in the region's rural counties]... is comprised of people 45 years of age or older. Rural farm counties contain the largest number of senior citizens (by percentage) of any county type, nearly twice that of metropolitan counties."[15]

[13]The specific counties visited will not be identified in this report. A number of respondents were concerned that their identities could be determined just through a description of their occupations and county location. However, they reside in seven of the 51 counties described as "rural farm" counties that meet the characteristics described in this text.

[14]These characteristics are largely drawn from Jon M. Bailey and Kim Preston, *Swept Away: Chronic Hardship and Fresh Promise on the Rural Great Plains: A Socio-Economic Study of the Rural Great Plains* (Walthill, Nebraska: Center for Rural Affairs, June 2003).

[15]Bailey and Preston, 8.

- *Great and widespread poverty:* The poverty rate in the rural farm counties of Nebraska is 12 percent, compared to 9 percent in the metropolitan regions of the state. Annual average per capita incomes are about 76 percent of such incomes in the metropolitan counties — $21,403 versus $28,115. While there has historically been an income gap between rural and urban areas, the gap has been widening.[16]
- *Reliance on unearned income:* Throughout the Great Plains region, 41 percent of per capita income is from unearned sources, such as Social Security, not surprising in an aging population. Earned income is barely half that of metropolitan counties.
- *Persistent downward trends in earnings and income:* Whether the agricultural year is good or bad for ranchers and farmers, regional earnings remain lower and trail those of metropolitan residents significantly.[17]

The picture of work in this region is also distinctive and marked by two features. There is *strong dependence on multiple job holding and part-time work.* Nebraska ranks first in the nation in the percentage of its workforce holding more than one job — 10.4 percent, and this characteristic was strongly exemplified by the work lives of the respondents in this study.

At the same time, the growth rate in Nebraska's small rural farm counties for the period 1990 to 2000 was the lowest in the Great Plains region, due to limited growth in wage and salary jobs. Not only are the jobs created in new sectors limited, but also the region is facing reductions in traditional work due to the *decline of farming jobs* resulting from farm consolidation and technological innovation. The National Governors Association Center for Best Practices notes that these trends caused "rural farm employment to fall from nearly 2.5 million in 1975 to around 1.8 million in 1996 — a 26.9 percent drop. Globalization of commodity markets and shrinking profit margins in traditional crops also has contributed to this decline. While these entities are important to rural economies, they typically support fewer jobs and businesses in the regions where they are located. The effect ... often is called 'hollowing out,' a process by which the business base erodes as fewer local products and services are purchased by a shrinking number of farmers."[18] The results of this trend are seen in the town centers of these counties. The number of stores is limited; vacant buildings sit among occupied stores; and some towns struggle to maintain a grocery store and other services.

This has led to a *strong dependence on entrepreneurial activities to fill the gap.* Forty-two percent of the jobs in the region's rural farm counties are sole proprietorships, and this figure includes more than just ranch and farm owners. In fact, "non-farm proprietorships are where much of the job growth is occurring in agriculturally-

---

[16]Bailey and Preston. Note that in the 1988-97 period, rural farm county per capita income was 85 percent of metropolitan counties. The gap by 2000 had increased by 9 percent.

[17]Bailey and Preston, 12, report that: "At the beginning of the decade, the average person in rural farm counties earned 58 percent of the average person in the metropolitan counties. By 2000, the average rural farm county resident earned only 48 cents of every dollar earned by a metropolitan county resident. The findings of previous studies showed that the disparity is chronic — the annual per capita earnings of agricultural communities fell below non-farm and metropolitan counties in 1976 and have remained lower ever since."

[18]"Innovative State Policy Options to Promote Rural Economic Development," NGA Center for Best Practices, Issue Brief, Economic and Technology Policy Studies, February, 2003, 2-3.

based counties." In Nebraska's rural farm counties, "non-farm self-employment represented about 67 percent of job growth ..."[19]

While this business activity is, on the one hand, a symptom of the lack of other job opportunities, it is also a reflection of the inherent capacity for independent work and entrepreneurial action that exists in the study area. The informal activities described by respondents are part and parcel of this drive to generate economic return in an area of scarce opportunity.

The Respondents

The respondents for this study were selected through a purposive sampling methodology aimed at achieving maximum variation in the cases selected for interview. Individuals were recruited by a local entrepreneur active in community economic development, familiar with the target area and with enterprise work in Nebraska. Interested individuals were screened by the recruiter and research team to select respondents who met a set of criteria, most importantly that they be adults between 20 and 65 years of age, low income, and engaged in informal economic activity currently or substantially over the last 12 months. The intent was to be equally inclusive of men and women and representative of a broad array of informal work activities.[20]

The sample that emerged from this screening included a diverse array of respondents in terms of economic activity, levels of experience and engagement in it, and economic goals. Nevertheless, they can be divided into two general groups — those who are part of ranch households or are aspiring ranchers, and townspeople whose work was indirectly connected to the ranch economy.

Ranching Households

This group represented 45 percent of the sample and included women and men who either considered ranching their principal economic activity, or who were working to make it the centerpiece of their economic livelihood. Among this group of individuals were men and women who headed ranching families and owned both ranch land and cattle, others who worked the ranch for elderly parents and anticipated assuming control once one generation passed to the next, others still who managed ranches for hire and were saving for their own properties, and individuals who owned cattle and ranched them on others' lands.

The ranch owners were all small holders who loved their work and the life that came with it. Most spoke eloquently about the land and their animals and the beauty of a lifestyle that kept them close to nature and near communities that they considered safe and wholesome. Compared to urban informal entrepreneurs, these individuals were much better positioned economically. If nothing else, ranch land is an asset of great value in this region. On the other hand, property is no guarantee that a family's annual income will place it in the middle class in any given year. Some ranchers spoke of downsizing herds and even selling them off in the last few years as they struggled to make ends meet. Others noted that cattle prices can vary

[19]Bailey and Preston, 16 and 31.

[20]For more on the research methodology, please see Appendix A.

from year to year and how it wouldn't take much to send their earnings sharply downwards. Ranchers, like farmers, are keenly aware of the risks of their profession, and the events of the last year demonstrated what those risks can be.

These ranchers believe they create a quality product and see themselves the stewards of the land. They are hardy, strong and resourceful individuals who, nonetheless, feel prey to market and environmental forces over which they can exercise little control. The only ways to mitigate the risks in this livelihood that they love, at least as they perceive it, are through saving in the good times and engaging in multiple economic activities, ranch-based and non-ranch.[21]

The aspiring ranchers included men and women who did not have title to ranch land but who were working towards it. In some cases, they were building herds that they kept on leased or borrowed lands; in others, they were working property with a view to purchasing it at a future point in time. Despite the hardships inherent in the life and the likely struggles ahead, this was the life they wanted to make with their families. Most worked untold hours and multiple jobs, and felt that with time they could earn enough to gain some property.

The Ups and Downs of Cattle Prices

After a long period of low prices (ascribed to competition from imports and a reduced emphasis on red meat in the American diet), things were looking up. Prices for cattle soared in October 2003, as American beef grew in demand in response to the appearance of Mad Cow disease in Canada. With the border closed to Canadian imports, not only in the U.S., but also around the world, U.S. producers found their product in higher demand. Compared to $66.76 per hundred-weight the previous year, cattle were selling for $108.80 the week of October 13, and the impact was already felt in the local supermarket. The cattle industry was also hopeful that the trend would continue with the increasing popularity of the Atkins Diet and others like it that emphasized protein consumption. But then, on December 23, 2003, Mad Cow disease was discovered in the U.S. as well, stunning the U.S. market. Just as Canada had experienced, import markets closed against the U.S. and prices declined. By January 2004, the USDA was projecting that prices would range between $72 to $78 per hundred-weight, and that U.S. beef exports would fall by 90 percent this year — from 2.6 billion pounds to just 220 million pounds — after virtually all foreign countries except Canada banned U.S. beef because of Mad Cow fears. The impact on the domestic market remained unclear.

*National Weekly Cattle and Beef Summary, USDA Livestock and Grain Market News, http://www.ams.usda.gov/mnreports/lm ct150.txt. "U.S. Mad Cow case to cut 2004 cattle prices — USDA," Reuters Report to Forbes.com, 01.12.04, 8:52AM ET., Available from http://www.forbes.com/home_europe/newswire/2004/01/12/rtr1206844.html; Internet.

[21]Another risk-mitigating technique might be to engage in alternative forms of cattle production, often called organic or sustainable ranching. In these models, cattle are strictly grass fed and not subjected to the hormone and antibiotic treatments that the majority of U.S. cattle face. But this is not an easy path for ranchers to take, given the relative newness and small size of market channels for organic beef. On the other hand, continued concern about corporate feedlots and slaughterhouse methods might increase demand for this product and encourage more small holders to try. For more on the challenges of this method, see "Story of a Steak," *Food and Wine,* November 2003; available from http://www.foodandwine.com/invoke.cfm?objectid=EFA8B641-6A00-4436-89A78195CDDF80F0; Internet.

The Townspeople

These individuals lived in and around the small towns that served as centers for the rural counties surrounding them. The townspeople worked for the county roads department, for seasonal recreational facilities, and for the school system as cafeteria workers and janitors. Some worked for motels out along the Interstate and others traveled long distances to work at a Wal-Mart distribution center. In addition to these sometimes part-time, sometimes full-time jobs, they would clean homes, watch children, do bookkeeping, make and sell crafts and foods, make ranch gear, work as ranch hands (called day workers) and break horses.

Their town centers contained grocery stores, post offices, banks, county courthouses and schools. Depending on the size of the community, they had cultural institutions like libraries, churches and community centers. At least two had historic buildings of tourist interest. One had a nursing home of some size. Most had at least one eating establishment and gas station, and a hotel or motel. There were no medical services. Shopping facilities were scant, and even in the larger towns, struggling. As one resident who had purchased the hardware store a year ago noted, the stores in these towns found it almost impossible to compete against Wal-Mart and other large chains found in the nearest major city. Used by townspeople as convenience stores rather than primary shopping destinations, they were hard pressed to survive, no matter the retail strategy. Townspeople, like ranchers, saved their major shopping for excursions to the biggest nearby cities.

The limited economic life of the town put constraints on the informal economic opportunities of the respondents. Some found an answer in providing services to older residents or to better-off homeowners. Others found it in selling crafts to a small market of interested neighbors and friends. Few had tried to expand their markets to communities or regions beyond their own.

A Statistical Profile

Table 1 summarizes the characteristics of the sample in quantitative terms. As can be seen, the sample contains 29 individuals of whom seven were male (24 percent of the sample) and 22 were female (76 percent of the sample).[22] Forty-five percent of the group is between 31 and 45 years old, while another 41 percent is between 46 and 60. All of the interviewees are white.

The sample's educational experience is high. Fully 79 percent of the sample has education beyond a high school diploma, and 31 percent have an associate's degree or above. Despite these high levels of education, their income levels place them at or below the low-income threshold for their county using HUD guidelines.[23] Fourteen percent reported incomes below $20,000 a year. Fifty-two percent had

---

[22]This skew in the proportion of male and female respondents is mitigated by the fact that the interviews covered the economic activities of all household members. Respondents reported on formal and informal work undertaken by both the men and women in the households. As most were married, the picture gained from these interviews is of both genders' economic roles in the informal economy.

[23]The Department of Housing and Urban Development publishes annual income guidelines that identify the median income for all metropolitan statistical areas and non-metropolitan counties in the country. Income limits are based on HUD estimates of median family income, with adjustments for family size. Low-income residents are considered those whose income, based on household size, is at or below 80 percent of the median income for the area. For more, see www.huduser.org; Internet. The researchers also interviewed an additional 13 individuals who did not meet this low-income threshold, but whose ability to stay "above the line" depended on their careful organization of a set of formal and informal work activities. While these individuals are not the primary subject of this document, these interviews added context and perspective to the reports from the low-income respondents.

incomes between $20,000 and $30,000. Twenty-one percent had incomes above this level.

The majority of the respondents are married. Only three individuals (10 percent of the sample) are divorced, separated or single. Household size ranges from one to six. The average and median household size is three. Most respondents live in households with a spouse or partner who is economically active, and in most instances, they live in homes of their own.

Table 1: Respondent Characteristics

	TOTAL	PERCENT*
Number of Respondents	29	100%
Male	7	24%
Female	22	76%
Age		
20-30	3	10%
31-45	13	45%
46-60	12	41%
61 and over	1	3%
Ethnicity		
White	29	100%
Education Level		
Some secondary	2	7%
High school grad or GED	4	14%
Some college-technical degree	14	48%
2-year degree	4	14%
4-year degree	5	17%
Marital Status		
Married/Living with partner	26	90%
Divorced/Separated	2	7%
Single	1	3%
Household Size		
1	1	3%
2	9	31%
3-4	12	41%
5 or more	7	24%
Annual Household Income[24]		
$12,000-$15,000	2	7%
$15,001-$20,000	2	7%
$20,001-$25,000	8	28%
$25,001-$30,000	7	24%
$30,001-$35,000	4	14%
$35,001-$40,000	2	7%
Unknown	4	14%

*Percentages not totaling 100 percent are due to rounding.

[24]Household income was reported by clients and reflected the revenues generated from each income stream into the household. In the case of ranching households where the respondents had difficulty reporting their income from the activity, an estimate was made based on the number of head of cattle that the rancher had, and using a net income figure estimated by Professor Barry Dunn of South Dakota State University. His study presents estimated profit per head of cattle for ranchers he defined as high, medium and low profit generating. The figure for "medium profit" generating was used. This group produces $36 in profit per cow as compared to a "high profit" group of ranchers who can generate $225 per cow, and a "low profit" group who lose up to $247 per cow. For more, please see Barry H. Dunn, "Measuring Cow-Calf Profitability and Financial Efficiency," (South Dakota State University, 2003, photocopied), 7.

Informal Work in Rural Communities

If there's one clear finding regarding rural participation in the informal economy, it's that it's a long-standing and extremely common approach to making a living. Making a little money "on the side" or exchanging services is an accepted tradition based on the economic realities of ranching. And, this informal work takes a variety of forms, including providing one's labor for hire on a cash basis or bartering it for goods and services; a range of supplementary self-employment activities that provide small and often irregular or seasonal flows of income into the household; and some microenterprises that the owners would identify and describe as businesses with growth possibilities. But, those described as businesses are few. The size of the activities, at least in terms of their economic return and their position within a household economic portfolio, make that perspective understandable. Most of these informal economy participants see what they're doing as just one more way to make a living and rarely speak in business terms about the activity. Jessica, a baker who sold her goods at shops and businesses in and near her hometown, expressed that point of view when she remarked: *"Actually, this has not started out as a business. That was not my intention. To me this is survival. Something for me to get by each week until I have a clearer direction as to what I am supposed to do with my life. I have dreams and goals to do something that's more than baking."* In that way she and other respondents are like many emerging microentrepreneurs who haven't applied a set of business concepts to their efforts. The way they work, layering one activity on top of the other as time and opportunity present, and shifting by season, conditions their estimation of the value of these efforts and their future prospects.

Patching As the Norm

Harriet does graphic design and printing on her home computer for a small number of individual clients and local businesses, and when called, provides back-up services for the local postmaster. Mike takes school and rodeo photos, does woodworking, and works at a bait and tackle store. And, Robin cleans several houses, mows lawns in the summer, sells her labor to a large ranch at peak work periods, and makes leather crafts in her spare time.

Like other microentrepreneurs and informal economy workers, the respondents in this study are patchers.[25] They combine informal work activities with formal jobs, as Harriet does. They also combine one or more informal work activities or businesses with others, as Robin does. Some of these patches are seasonal; some represent part-time income streams that flow into the household throughout the

[25]Patching is a term used to describe the multiple economic activities that one individual engages in to generate an income. In addition, a household may have other income streams contributed by other household members.

year, although not necessarily at the same income level. In all, the 29 low-income respondents interviewed reported engaging in 51 formal and 39 informal activities. Only one informal business was reported to be full time. These are very busy individuals who work extremely hard to make a living.

But, they are not the only ones who are busy. In many instances, their spouses[26] also engage in multiple activities. Respondents described household economic portfolios[27] that contained three, five, seven and eight economic activities (the mode for the group was four) operated in most instances by only two individuals.

The pie charts on this page and the next present two examples of what this looks like. The first example illustrates the case of Judith and her husband, who have grown children and now live on their own in one of the small towns that dot the rural countryside.

6 Activities

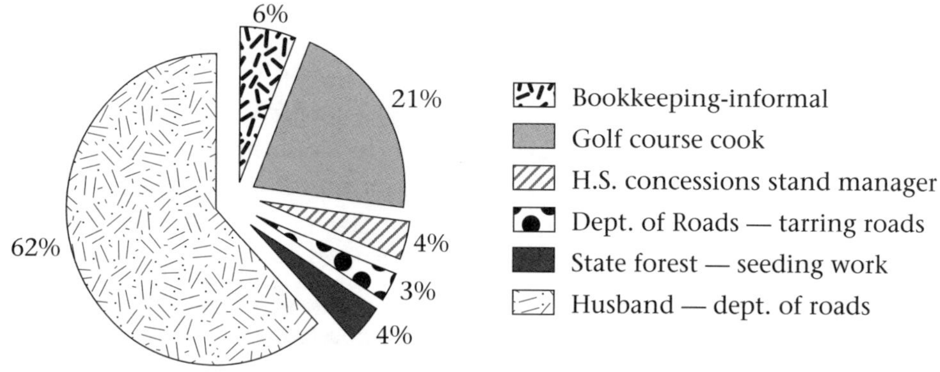

Almost two-thirds of their income is generated by the husband's job with the county roads department. He is the shop foreman, earning a little over minimum wage for his efforts. Judith brings in the rest of their income through a series of activities, most of which are formal and seasonal. Informally throughout the year, Judith is a bookkeeper for a long-distance trailer driver from their community who spends most of the year on the road. He depends on her to manage his financial recordkeeping and maintain all his proper licensing with the various states through which he drives. It's complex, detailed work that Judith loves, having grown up with a father who was also a trailer driver. She spends about 14 hours a month on this work, which she enjoys more than all her other occupations. Unfortunately,

[26]Almost all respondents reported themselves as married. Only two said they were divorced or separated, and one was single.

[27]A household economic portfolio can be defined as "a) a set of household resources [including human, physical and financial], b) the set of household activities [including consumption, production and investment], and c) the circular flow of interaction between household resources and household activities." Within the portfolio, households "rearrange over time their mix of resources, labor and economic activities to cope with changing economic and social objectives or contingencies." This conceptualization of a household's economic life was developed by Martha Alter Chen and Elizabeth Dunn for the USAID-funded AIMS Project (Assessing the Impact of Microenterprise Services), and was applied to the examination of low-income households engaged in microenterprise in developing countries, and helped to both describe their activities and understand the complexity of joint and individual economic decision-making and juggling that enabled these low-income families to survive. The model is equally applicable to the rural households that are the subjects of this research, which are characterized by multiple income streams, some managed by individuals and some (like the ranch) which may be jointly operated (if not managed). Economic activities are regularly adjusted to take advantage of opportunities as they emerge. For more on this model, see Chen and Dunn, *Household Economic Portfolios*, (Washington, D.C.: U.S. Agency for International Development, AIMS, 1996); available from http://www.usaidmicro.org/pubs/pubsTemplate.asp?page=/componen/aims/pubs/english/desk7.htm; Internet.

there are few opportunities available to a skilled bookkeeper where she lives, so she works as a cook at the local golf course from spring through fall, earning most of the income she contributes to the household. She also works briefly each year for the state forestry service packing seedlings for distribution outside the state. Additionally, she drives heavy equipment during tarring season for the same county roads department that employs her husband. Combined these five activities contribute under $8,000 to the household.

The second case is of another woman, Laura, and her husband. There are four in their household, and while they don't own a ranch, a large portion of their income comes from ranch-related activities.

8 ACTIVITIES

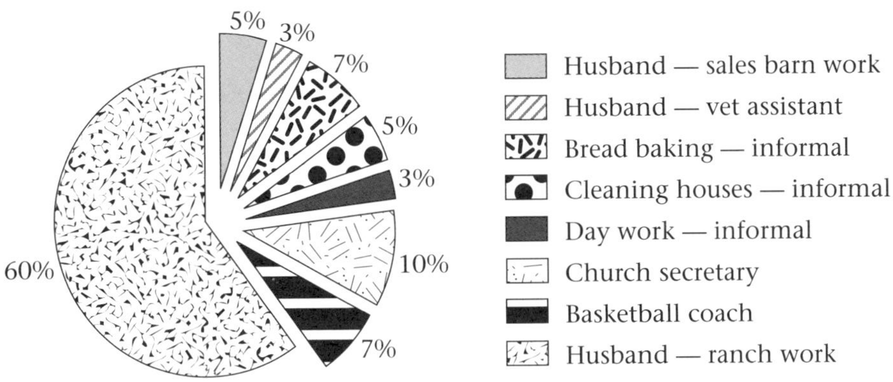

Laura and her husband live and work on a ranch owned by an older widowed gentleman who moved to town. They manage his land and cattle, and own a few head of their own. An informal agreement covers their work arrangement and how the revenues will be shared. However, because the ranch is very small and will not sustain both the owner and their family, Laura's husband also works at the sales barn once or twice a month and as an assistant to a veterinarian when asked. Both he and Laura also do "day work," working as ranch hands at local ranches when the season demands. In addition, Laura has two formal jobs: she provides secretarial services for her church about 30 hours a month, and coaches the girl's high school basketball team four months a year. Informally, she also sells homemade whole wheat bread at the farmers' market in the summer and to individual customers throughout the rest of the year. Altogether these eight activities generate an income that is classified as low-income, according to HUD standards for their county.

These two illustrations demonstrate several aspects of this working lifestyle. First, in the lives of these respondents and the others interviewed, the informal activities generally represent a small proportion of the household's income. Earnings ranged from a low of $0 to a high of $12,350.[28] The contribution they made to annual household earnings also ranged from 0 percent to 59 percent.[29] The median was 13 percent and the average was 17 percent. The informal activities in

[28]One respondent reported that her business generated no earnings for the household in the last year. This was a struggling horse training and riding center. Not including her, the minimum annual reported earnings were $120.

[29]Without the horse center business, the minimum percent contribution to the household was two percent.

almost every case were designed to be a portion of individual and household income, and even when interest was expressed in growing the business, only a few expressed interest in having that activity become a full-time occupation. Additional revenue was the goal, but rarely was it envisioned that the activity would replace other activities undertaken by the respondent. There were two principal reasons for this:

- In the case of ranch households, the ranch is the centerpiece of the household's economic portfolio. All other activities are developed in and around the ranching cycle. Other economic activities are undertaken to help maintain the family in ranching, to generate additional revenue to support the growth of the ranch, or, in the case of aspiring ranchers, to generate savings that would allow a household to purchase cattle or land. Robin expressed that perspective well when she said, *"Our ideal dream is both to just stay at home and ranch, but, unfortunately, things don't meet, so we've had to spread ourselves and do a lot of different things to make it work."*
- In many cases — both for ranch families and non-ranch families — the need for benefits and a constant stream of income lead people to value and hold onto formal employment. As Kate noted, *"I worked the weekend shift down at the distribution center, because there were the benefits: the insurance, the health insurance, because ... when you ranch you have to have health insurance, just because if you don't, you don't know whether you are going to be able to survive or not."*

Among the respondents, two major sources of jobs with benefits were identified: the state and county roads departments and Wal-Mart's new distribution center in North Platte. The distribution center was a fairly new employer in the region, having opened in March 2003. Several respondents reported that the opportunity to work for the center caused a change in their mix of economic activities. Some had reduced their informal work to accommodate their part- or full-time schedule at Wal-Mart, considering this a much better option for the family despite the demands it placed on them in terms of the structure of the work.[30]

A second factor constraining the size of these informal economic activities may be the attitude of the respondents toward such work. Many appeared to have a heightened awareness of, and sensitivity to, the illegal character of their non-reporting of income. Jessica, for example, stated: *"I am aware of what you can make a year and be within the legal guidelines ... What I've been told; it is $600 a year. I know I have exceeded that."* Most respondents justified the non-reporting because of the size of the earnings and sometimes because of their irregularity. They also justified operating in an informal way precisely because the activities were small. If the activities grew in size, then the terms under which they operated would, in their minds, have to change. More on their perceptions will be presented in the next chapter.

[30]Respondents who had obtained jobs at the distribution center reported receiving wages approximating $13.50 an hour, which was a substantially higher wage than that received by many others in the study. (The most frequently reported wage was $8.00 an hour.) To earn that wage and the benefits that accompanied it, respondents reported working at least three 12-hour shifts during the week. Because of the distances involved, at least one respondent's spouse stayed in a motel for two nights each week to accommodate the schedule. One respondent who chose not to pursue a position at Wal-Mart spoke of the conflict that such a long schedule would create with both childrearing and ranching responsibilities.

Layering of Activities

One of the singular characteristics of these respondents was their ability to see and fit money-making opportunities in the interstices between formal work and/or other obligations. While some described a common pattern of a summer job between yearly stints as a cafeteria worker or maintenance worker in a school system, others described a much more complex layering of activities across the year. The strategy entails fitting in extra jobs or work around a variety of other fixed obligations in a way that efficiently uses up available "downtime." Glen, for example, works daily for the county roads, and makes halters in the evenings while watching television or spending time with family. He also breaks horses for people, fitting that work into the mornings before work and on the weekends. Becky sells bread at farmers' markets in the summer, but also runs an off-season "bread route" delivering bread to customers in the city in conjunction with regular shopping trips there. Dustin takes photos at high school rodeos he attends to see his grandchildren, and offers them for sale. Still other women, kept close to the ranch because of ranch chores and children, use spare time to prepare jellies that are sold at summertime farmers' markets. The jellies are made across a period of months to take advantage of less busy periods.

There is a real seasonal nature to the ebb and flow of many of these activities. Not surprisingly, for some the dynamic of the ranch seasons governs how other work fits. But, even townspeople can have seasonal flows to their work. Below are two case examples of what this can look like for a household.

Laura and her husband, the couple who lived on and managed a ranch for an absentee owner, are both patchers, basing their income on a variety of stable and irregular work activities. Juggling a set of activities across the year provides them cash-flow during the long ranching season. It also provides them a cushion against the possibility of low cattle prices in the fall. Their household portfolio includes ranch work and off-farm formal work, informal labor for hire activities, and an informal bread-baking business. Steady year-round activities are enhanced with seasonal efforts that relate to the school and agricultural cycle. But, this way of working can be exhausting: *"I would stay up all night Friday baking bread. I mean, some I would take out of the oven at 2 or 4 in the morning, and I would be at the farmers' market at 6:00,"* reported Laura. Another respondent, Kate, who worked similarly, noted, *"Just like the pies, who else would be crazy enough to ... go to bed at 2 or 3 o'clock in the morning and turn around and get up at 4 in the morning, so you get about two/three hours of sleep. You do what you have to do to survive."* This is the price western Nebraskan residents pay to keep their heads above water.

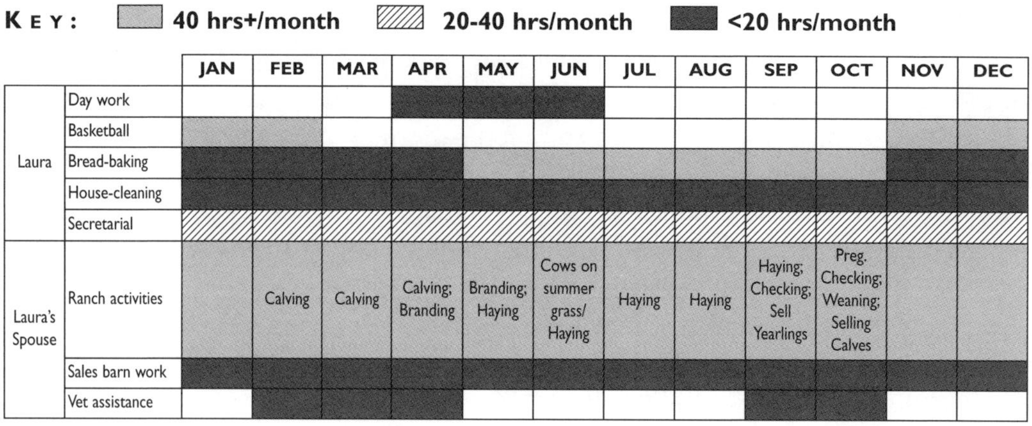

Ranch families aren't the only ones who layer activity upon activity. Pete and his wife live in town, engaging in eight different activities across the year to keep their household of four going. Eschewing a job that would leave him tied to a single activity, Pete prefers to alternate five different activities, several of which ebb and flow with the seasons. While a few of his activities are year-round, they generally require a minimal amount of time every month. This frees him to spend more concerted time on seasonal activities, as well as be with his family in their family mowing business and participate in his children's activities. His wife noted, *"Pete isn't really a nine-to-five kind of guy. He likes the flexibility of being able to mow a lawn one day here, go to a funeral the next day, and just [have] the ability to make your own schedule."* Whether he could find a single job that would generate the same amount of income as these is also questionable.

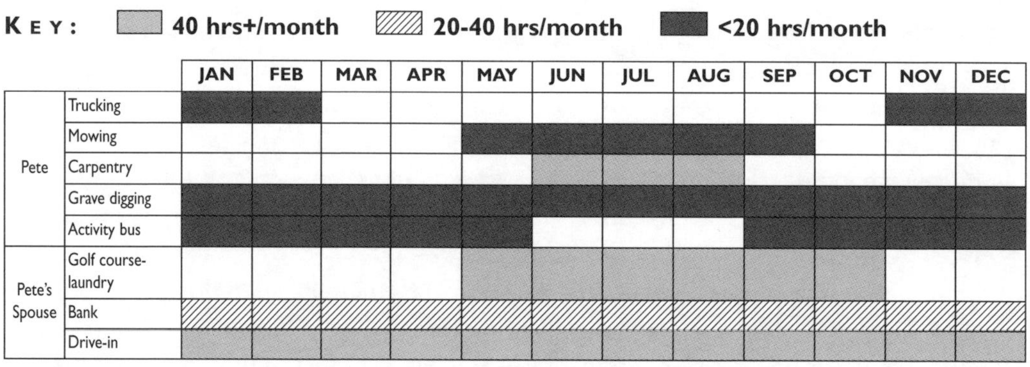

This type of working requires great juggling skills and an ability to work hard for sustained periods of time. On the other hand, the result is that most activities remain very small contributors to the household.

Low Business Returns and Business Assets

Not including their day work and bartering activities, the respondents managed 39 different business activities. Of these, only one was full time. The median annual earnings reported for each activity was $3,250 and the average was $4,061.[31] This represents a median contribution of 16 percent to the overall household income, or 19 percent on average per activity. Of course, the overall contribution of informal revenue in a household is higher in some instances when the income of all informal activities is combined. One respondent, Jessica, generated 59 percent of her income from an informal business. Other households garnered as much as 23 and 30 percent from informal sources.

The value of reported assets was generally low as well. The median value of reported assets was $900 and the average was $3,364. The range was from $0 to $15,600. The businesses with no reported assets included a few home-based food businesses that reported only using personal kitchen/cooking items, and a couple of cleaning businesses for which the owners reported using their personal vacuums and cars. At the high end was a photography business in which the owner had very recently invested in digital equipment to increase the range of jobs he could take, and carpentry and woodworking businesses which the owners indicated used a large number of tools purchased over time.

The size of these businesses in terms of earnings is small relative to informal businesses operating in urban settings. As an example, interviews with Latino informal entrepreneurs, both documented and undocumented, found that their median and average annual earnings were $6,840 and $9,504 respectively. Similarly, the average earnings for African American informal entrepreneurs were $12,156. In these instances, the informal enterprises were a much larger part of the overall household's income. In the case of the Latino entrepreneurs, the median percentage contribution to household income was 54 percent and the average was 60 percent. In the case of the African Americans interviewed, only 18 percent reported having any formal work (10 of 55 respondents).[32] This greater dependence on the informal business is not surprising on the part of the Latinos whose other resources (in the form of educational attainment, property and, in many instances, legal status) were more limited than those of the rural respondents. And, African American informal economy participants seemed more drawn to informal work for a mix of reasons, including the inability to secure formal employment or dissatisfaction with past experiences in the job market.

On the other hand, the rural respondents were more likely to have the ranch or a formal job as the centerpiece of their economic activities. The drive to engage in

[31]These numbers should be understood as rough estimates. They were derived through a series of questions with each respondent, asking what their earnings were from the businesses during the months in which they operated. Depending on the type of business, respondents reported weekly or monthly figures, or sometimes figures by the job (for example, the average revenue per school photo shoot and the number of "shoots" during the school picture-taking season. Respondents were also asked to consider low and peak periods of earnings as they reported their returns. Some respondents were able to report precise figures based on their own recordkeeping. Others were more imprecise. In all cases, the number requested was their earnings after paying for materials and other business-related expenses, such as renting tables at farmers' markets. It was what they considered their return to labor. These earnings were not reduced to reflect "hidden" expenses such as the cost of utilities used in producing their product, vehicle repairs or other non-cash expenses, such as depreciation. In this respect, then, most earnings should be considered overestimated.

[32]Edgcomb and Armington, *The Informal Economy: Latino Enterprises at the Margins,* (Washington, D.C.: The Aspen Institute/FIELD, 2003), 26: Losby, Kingslow and Else, *The Informal Economy: Experiences of African Americans,* (Washington, D.C.: The Aspen Institute, 2003), 31.

informal work was more for risk mitigation and income supplementation. In an environment where ranching returns varied greatly from year to year and where most paying jobs were at the low end of the income scale, small informal activities carried an importance to the worker or owner beyond the total dollars and cents earned. As Robin pointed out: *"It's just all those things that if it wasn't for all my little jobs, there would be no way we could ranch and survive ... Oh, it's very important, I mean, that's one key to survive. That's how the groceries get on the table."*

Table 2: Respondent Businesses

	TOTAL	PERCENT*
Total respondents	29	100%
Total businesses	39	
Full time	1	3%
Part time	38	97%
Business Type		
Photography	3	8%
Salon services	1	3%
Cakes	2	5%
Lawn care	2	5%
Odd jobs	1	3%
Woodworking	2	5%
Ranch gear	2	5%
Horse breaking/training	3	8%
Arts and crafts	5	13%
Animal raising/trapping	4	10%
Specialty foods	7	18%
Child care	2	5%
Bookkeeping	1	3%
Office/house cleaning	4	10%
Annual Business Earnings[33]		
Minimum	$ 120	
Maximum	$12,350	
Median	$ 3,250	
Average	$ 4,048	
Business Assets		
Minimum	$ –	
Maximum	$15,600	
Median	$ 900	
Average	$ 3,364	
Business Income as Percent of Household Income		
Minimum	2%	
Maximum	59%	
Median	14%	
Average	18%	

[33]The reported earnings do not include those of one entrepreneur who reported drawing nothing from her business last year. With her included, the minimum drops to $0, the median to $3,000, and the average to $3,908.

Table 2: Respondent Businesses (continued)

	TOTAL	PERCENT*
Interested in Growing Business		
Yes	18	62%
No	10	34%
Maybe	1	3%
Interested in Loan		
Yes	6	21%
No	20	69%
Maybe	2	7%
Unknown	1	3%
Would Prefer Stable Job to Microenterprise		
Yes	7	24%
No	18	62%
Maybe	4	14%

*Percentages not totaling 100 percent are due to rounding.

Table 3: Respondent Informal Work Activities

	TOTAL	PERCENT
Total respondents	29	100%
Total informal work activities	3	
Full time	0	0%
Part time	3	100%
Type of Work		
Rodeo/4-H judging	1	33%
Day work	2	67%
Annual Earnings		
Minimum	$ 184	
Maximum	$ 5,040	
Median	$ 840	
Average	$ 2,021	
Informal Activity Income as Percent of Household Income		
Minimum	1%	
Maximum	21%	
Median	3%	
Average	8%	

A Closer Look at Rural Informal Work

As the previous chapter indicated, informal economy participants in western Nebraska are characterized by their engagement in multiple, very small-scale economic activities. Supreme jugglers, these individuals go from one enterprise to the next, accommodating each in a work schedule that seems endless. This chapter will explore in greater detail the motivations that drive these individuals to work in this way and to operate informally. It will also present a typology of these informal work activities, defined by both their characteristics and future prospects.

Motivations

"We're diverse, because you have to be in this area."
— Jody

There are at least four motivations that underlie the multi-tasking and dependence on informal work that is a normal part of the work life of these respondents. They include:

- *Risk mitigation:* Especially in an area dependent on ranching and agricultural income, where many factors outside one's control influence the ultimate economic return, there is a strong need to have other income sources flowing into the household. In some instances, respondents spoke explicitly about the other economic activities being the support that enables them to stay in ranching at all. In other instances, the additional activities were portrayed as essential for cash-flow, when the primary activity — the ranch — operated on an annual cycle with an uncertain payoff. *"When there's a drought, you do whatever you can do to bring in more income, and that's why we tried this. I don't think anybody in the rural areas has just one job, they do two or three to try to make it."*— Rose
- *Lack of other good employment opportunities:* While some respondents are formally employed, formal jobs are limited, so people interested in generating additional cash need to be creative and draw on their own talents or skills to generate work where there was none before. This work can also serve to fill gaps in the local retail scene. They make cakes to order in towns that don't have bakeries; they photograph students in communities without photography studios; and they run pre-schools where such enrichment educational experiences are lacking. They meet needs in communities that can't sustain more full-scale permanent operations that in other locales might be their employers, and in so doing create their own work. At the same time,

the fragility of these markets limits the growth of the enterprises, and therefore, forces them to continue to add activities rather than grow just one.

Creating a Home-based Pre-school

When Tara's oldest turned four, Tara decided to run her own home-based pre-school. A former teacher, Tara prized early childhood education and wanted to give her children the experience of *"circle time and story time and just some regimented structure time during the day."* But, the nearest pre-schools were in the large city center some 40 miles away. Between the tuition and the travel, getting her daughter to an established pre-school seemed daunting. At the same time, she had the skills and experience to create a quality experience for her children. A mother of three, Tara was already operating a regulated day care, caring for up to three children in addition to her own at home. In addition, she had six years of early childhood teaching experience behind her. She decided to hold a pre-school program two mornings a week for a small group of children.

Tara did an informal survey of the price of attending pre-school in neighboring towns, cut the price in half and subtracted out a little more to come up with the price of $28 per month per child for her pre-school. Tara *"basically just tried to think what we could afford to pay"* to send their own child to pre-school, and assumed others in her area would be willing to pay a similar amount.

Tara had about five children formally involved in the pre-school, including her oldest daughter. In addition, her younger children and those under her day-care supervision also joined in to the extent that they could follow along with the activities. The pre-school met two mornings a week from 9:00 to 11:45. Because of extensive up-front investments, Tara didn't think she came out very far ahead in her pre-school's first year. She and her husband converted their garage to a family room that could be used for her day care and pre-school. She bought numerous books and educational materials and supplies. When asked how much she thought she invested in these materials, she replied, *"I don't want to know."* Nevertheless, Tara intends to continue the pre-school next year and thinks she'll recoup many of her expenses, not including, of course, the home improvement.

She plans to continue offering her pre-school as long as her children are pre-school age — another three years or so. She reported very positive feedback from the parents and *"found it rewarding to notice how much better (the children) cooperated … and just seeing the growth in them … academically too."*

Despite her success with this first experience and her plan to continue this year, Tara isn't sure that she'd ever set up a formal pre-school in her town. She notes: *"… I think in this area you're a little limited because of the distance people need to travel and because of the incomes being low, and although there are people here certainly who see the benefit, like, in a pre-school education … a lot of times, you know, people will just … obviously kind of teach them at home, and which can certainly be done and be done well, but the group socialization is something that is lost."* In addition, Tara looks ahead to other demands on her time. Her husband has an informal agreement to take over a ranch from an elderly gentleman where he now works as a manager. If and when this happens, Tara will have to decide whether to continue her day-care and pre-school activities or help her husband on the ranch full time.

- *Small-scale returns* for many of the activities engaged in, due to characteristics of their products/services or their markets, or both. Quilting, for example, is a high art that when done according to traditional methods is extremely time-intensive. There are just so many quilts an individual can make when she's also running a cleaning business or working on a ranch with her husband. At the same time, the return for such quilts locally is restricted by the low discretionary income available to inhabitants of the area. One quilter spoke of selling hand-made quilts for $200 to $300, and only recently having gone on the Internet to discover the higher prices such products command in the larger marketplace. Similarly jams and jellies are common products that women can easily do in their kitchens in limited quantities, but are not scalable without transforming the production process significantly. These products also meet strong price resistance in the local market, where many women know how to preserve. Horse breaking is yet another high-touch activity that involves the personal attention of the business owner, and while the skill of the trainer can affect price and demand to some extent, the fact is that the trainers can only work so many horses at any given time.

Bookkeeper for Hire

With bookkeeping experience dating back to high school, Judith started keeping books for an independent trucker about a year ago. He's a neighbor of hers, but is on the road 300 days a year. Her father was a trucker and she had kept the books for him as well for several years, building up specialized expertise in bookkeeping related to trucking, which is complicated due to all the filings truckers need to maintain with the states in which they operate. She keeps track of her hours and is paid $10 per hour. She enjoys the work because *"it can be done, most of it, can be done in a short period of time … I mean, sure, the insurance has to be paid by a certain date, but there is no real time schedule that has to be, so it works in with everything else."* (Everything else for Judith includes work at the golf course, managing the high school concession stand at games and events, and seasonal work with the county roads department and state forest.) She also enjoys it because it allows her to expand her knowledge and *"keeps me updated on different things. Not that I'll probably ever have to know … you know, licensing and fees for all these states."* In fact, Judith would like to expand her bookkeeping operations and has looked into providing her services to other truckers. She even took a Quicken class to be able to offer computerized bookkeeping services. Unfortunately she says, *"There is just not much demand for something like that right around here."* Judith explains that the few small businesses in the area do their own books rather than hiring the bookkeeping out. Oftentimes the wives of the business owners do the books for their husband business owners.

Judith believes *"The day of the independent trucker is about gone,"* further putting a damper on her bookkeeping dreams. Rising fuel, equipment and insurance costs have made it more difficult to be an independent owner/operator. Judith mentioned that the independent trucker she currently works for is thinking of working for Wal-Mart, and after looking into employment with the company, said, *"I don't know why I didn't do this years ago, because they pay insurance for retirement, all this, paid vacation." He says, "I have never had any of that as an independent driver."*

- *A desire to keep each activity within their management capacity:* Many respondents acknowledge that growth would raise a set of issues regarding the management of the business or its formalization that they don't feel prepared to address. For women to sell their foods through Grow Nebraska, a nonprofit microenterprise program that provides training and marketing assistance to crafters and specialty foods producers in the state, they would need to produce the foods in certified commercial kitchens.[34] None of the entrepreneurs interviewed felt they could justify investing in one on their own, nor did they feel that a cooperative venture would work given the distances between producers and a town center. Other entrepreneurs reported that they didn't have the desire or the management capacity to conduct their activities on a larger scale. Jody explained that her growth was limited by her lack of a business background *"because I don't have any formal business training; I do not like book work of any sort."* Similarly, Harriet commented, *"I am almost kind of scared, because I have never been in a business, never done a business before. I guess I am a little bit hesitant."* Understanding the regulations surrounding commercial kitchens were particularly cited as difficult obstacles. Kate explains how a commercial kitchen makes the idea of growth seem all but impossible. *"But your cost, the overhead of having a commercial kitchen ... you would have to have a commercial kitchen to do all these things. You would have to have the inspections and ... you cannot afford to do it."* Still others cite their family obligations or other job responsibilities as impediments to growth. Lisa

[34]Grassroots Resources and Opportunities for Winners (Grow) Nebraska is a nonprofit marketing and training program for Nebraska artisan businesses and home-based entrepreneurs. A membership organization, Grow Nebraska started accepting members in 1998. Members join Grow through an application and jury review process. Grow provides jury review of products, access to retail and wholesale markets, cooperative advertising through print and Internet media, and training opportunities to members. Grow has a partnership with the University of Nebraska Food Processing Center, where all food producers are referred for educational resources.

loves working outdoors and enjoys her lawn-mowing business. However, because of her family child-care constraints, she's had to turn down business. She would like to grow her business, *"but I doubt that I will because ... somebody would have to move in to help with my son, so I cannot take on too much work."*

Why Informality?

While the factors above influence the size of the activity, entrepreneurs cite additional reasons for keeping the business informal:

- Perhaps most importantly is the attitude of the individual toward the activity itself. Looked at as something that fits within other economic activities that they do, it's *seen less as a "business" than as just another way one works to make a little money.* As one more patch in a complex of economic endeavors, it isn't perceived as something that needs to be any more structured than the work itself requires. And, if it demanded more rigor in paperwork and other requirements, it would lose its value to the entrepreneur and his/her family. This is why the bread makers, jelly producers and noodle makers like Kate, Becky and Laura express concern regarding rumors of more regulation invading the farmers' markets where they sell. At what point would it be more hassle than the economic return they generate for the substantial labor they already invest in food preparation? *"You have to post a sign that 'these are not produced in a commercial kitchen,' in a non-inspected kitchen; you have to weigh everything. There are a lot of barriers ... that are hurting the small person, the small business trying to make a living."*— Kate
- Often the activity is *so small-scale (or occasional or erratic) that it's not worth reporting as far as the entrepreneur is concerned.* Neither Julie, who does occasional alterations for friends (earning about $365 a year), Marilyn who sells found farm objects as antiques (estimating her return at $200), nor Paul who caters a few barbecues now and then (maybe gaining $120), generate enough revenue from the activity to raise concerns on the part of the IRS. Despite the small returns, the activities are important to the respondents for many reasons. Although her returns were small, Marilyn explains that the business revenues *"are very important, because they go for extra things."* It's the money that makes the difference between just surviving and feeling like there's a little space for either emergencies or small pleasures. For Penny, however, the most important reason for her business was not the money. *"Part of the reason why I do it, is extra income is nice. But, more than that, I would go absolutely nuts being on the farm all by myself all day with two kids, you know. As much as I love them to pieces and I love being home ... I don't want to be just a wife or one that just sits home, because I know how hard my husband works."*
- There is a *tradition of exchange and barter* that continues in these communities, and while these exchanges may be calculated in rough terms to ensure that the trades are "even," rarely are records kept of these valuations. Rather the exchanges represent important inputs into households that can operate quite invisibly to the outside world and are attractive for that reason.

- Finally, in a few cases, *the activity is new and being tested* to see if it is worth converting into a larger or more formal operation. In these instances, the entrepreneur will increasingly move to following more of the rules of the game as the potential of the business becomes clearer. A few of these activities will be described below.

While there are strong reasons supporting informal work, the respondents' attitudes about their working this way are mixed. On the one hand, a few individuals spoke with real *impatience regarding the rules and regulations* that they felt made their work difficult or impeded their growth. This is certainly the perspective of the food producers who fear greater state control over how they're allowed to sell at farmers' markets. It is also the perspective of Robert who does carpentry work, among his many other jobs. Looking ahead to the possibility that he would have to collect sales taxes from his customers, he said:

> *"I think with this new sales tax law, it is going to become a bigger issue with the carpentry industry. Well, Nebraska is starting the first of October, and I'm trying to study up on it; I just learned about it. You're supposed to start charging (sales tax) for your labor. Well, so far it is just the carpentry business and electrical repairmen, and plumbers and things like that. I don't know a lot about that, but I think that that is going to make smaller people ... go to a cash business, which I don't know if that is going to be good or bad ... the bookkeeping issue is just going to be a nightmare. And, I do the bookkeeping, but if you consider your time worth anything, that means that you need to pass that on to people. Well, when you're in a small community like this, and people are on a fixed income, it's difficult. Because you either charge them more, or make less ..."*

At the same time, however, and even more strongly expressed in the interviews, respondents recorded *real discomfort* with operating informally. Some spoke in strongly ethical terms regarding what's right and wrong about an informal approach to generating an income and could justify their own behavior only because of the relatively small amounts of money involved. As Jessica explained, *"I realize, if it keeps growing that honesty is on the line; you have to report your income."*

Informal Economic Activities: Characteristics and Prospects

One of the principal questions this research asks is to what extent informal economy participants might be appropriate candidates for microenterprise program services. Behind that question are two others: which kinds of activities have the potential to grow and become larger scale contributors to household income? And, which kinds of individuals have the potential to become entrepreneurs and formal business owners? (Clearly there are some economic activities that could grow if the owner were so inclined, or freed from important household responsibilities or competing work obligations.) This section presents a categorization of the informal work conducted by the respondents, based on its likelihood to develop along a path with growth potential.

Informal Work

This category contains all those activities in which labor is exchanged for cash or for other products and services. In all instances, the labor is provided on an occasional basis depending on the seasonal or special needs of those who hire them. Among the respondents are found incidences of each of the following types of work:

- *"Day labor"* — This is the term used to describe the work of ranch hands who provide extra help to ranchers during peak ranching periods, such as when branding (April, May) or weaning (October) occur. Four individuals among the respondents and their spouses worked as day laborers, earning an average of around $75 per day. Day workers may work regularly with one rancher; others may sell their services to several as needed. For some, like Laura, it represents a small patch in their income (under $1,000 annually). For others, like Robin, it represents a much more substantial source of revenue (over $5,000).
- *Opportunistic work* — This describes work engaged in when the occasion to sell services arises. Marilyn who does regular summer judging at 4-H competitions is a prime example of this type of activity. But, it comes in other forms as well. The researchers encountered rodeo judges, basketball referees and special occasion singers, each of whom reported working for cash. Workers engaged in these endeavors often do it out of love for the activity as much as for the money it generates. When Laura was asked if she would give up some of her informal activities for more hours at a formal job, she hinted at the complexity behind the reasons to participate in so many economic activities. *"I might not be able to give those things up either, I'd probably do it for free, but I enjoy the payment for it. The basketball coaching, you know, I don't do it for the money either. I do it because I enjoy it."*
- *Work that is done for barter* — Services are exchanged for products or other services. These bartering arrangements can be ad hoc and imprecise in terms of establishing an equivalency of exchange, or they can be quite tightly controlled. Among the respondents engaged in barter were Debra, who offered young people riding lessons in exchange for their help in cleaning stables, and Robert, who managed a complex of trading relationships, exchanging tractor trailer driving and horse training for hay, and work at a lumber yard for lumber and other materials. Robert appeared to live as much of his economic life "off the grid" as possible, and delighted in the informal and free nature of these various interchanges. Diametrically opposed to this approach in spirit is another example of a bartering arrangement designed to insure that each side gets fair and full value for the services rendered, one that also involved Marilyn.

You do the books; I'll fix your tractor: A Bartering Arrangement

In the fall of 2002, Marilyn was talking to her closest neighbor, Jeff, about his auto-body mechanic shop. He had recently purchased a computer and intended to computerize his invoicing. Although his mother had been doing his bookkeeping, she decided not to continue after he bought his computer. As they began talking about computers, Marilyn mentioned that she and her husband were very familiar with Excel, having just completed a class on the software at the local community college. Jeff asked if she would be willing to learn QuickBooks Pro and handle his invoicing for him. Marilyn and her husband had a tractor and car at the neighbor's shop to be repaired, so she replied, *"I could probably do that, if you could trade for some mechanical work."*

Since they made this agreement, Marilyn has regularly worked for Jeff. At first, she only did monthly invoicing, spending about 8-10 hours on the work. As time has progressed though, she's encouraged him to put more of his business on the computer. Marilyn now does invoicing more frequently, as well as business statements and aging of accounts receivable. She feels it has helped Jeff's business, *"he was known before for taking three months to bill someone. His account receivables are current, except for one customer."* Marilyn and her husband have benefited too. *"We got several tractors repaired and an automobile serviced, and we have some more work that needs to be done."*

In order to make sure that the arrangement is fair, both Marilyn and Jeff track their hours and Jeff tracks his parts and expenses. *"By the end of the year, we'll add everything up and see who owes who. And, then pay the other person."* Marilyn and Jeff both set their hourly rates so this year-end accounting will be very straightforward.

The reality about all this work is that while it may be amenable to some growth and change (horse breaking and bookkeeping can be operated as an income-generating business; for example), most of this activity is likely to remain contingent and small in scale.

Supplementary Self-Employment or Microenterprise

What characterizes businesses of this type is generally their goal: they are designed to serve as income patches in the household and generally are intentionally limited in scale to fit with other economic activities. These businesses constituted the majority of the economic activities operated by the study respondents and included among them, enterprises in four sectors: arts and crafts, foods, services and animal-related industries.

The *arts and crafts businesses* in this cluster serve very local markets — friends, family, referrals, and occasional craft shows. Some of these activities are done at a fairly elementary level, and while they might satisfy local needs, could not compete in more competitive markets. They include the graphics printing done by Harriet, whose principal customers included a photographer of windmills (who put her artwork on simple note cards to be sold at coffee shops, gas stations and other locations where tourists might stop) and local businesses who ordered calendars that they distributed as part of their year-end publicity efforts. Others were of a higher end, such as Mike's woodworking efforts that involved picture frame making, and children's furniture and toy production; but, no one had attempted to reach larger or more affluent markets. These crafts were all time-intensive. While at least one respondent mentioned being involved in a local quilting club, there appeared to be no discussion of pooling efforts in a money-making endeavor. Although one entrepreneur reported earning $5,400 from her craft last year, the majority reported much lower earnings. The average was $1,656 and the median earnings were a lower $825. The assets invested in these businesses were also relatively low. While one woodworker reported about $8,000 invested in tools, the average was $2,551 and the median was $1,653.

The food businesses comprised a second category — makers of breads, pies, cakes, jellies, noodles and other goods. Most of these individuals were ranch wives and used farmers' markets as their principal marketing channel. A second smaller channel during the "off season" included bread routes constructed by the women to a select list of town-based customers to whom they delivered on weekly or biweekly trips to town. Most expressed that to grow these businesses would require stepping up to commercial kitchens, and none felt ready to make an individual investment in doing this. Current farmers' markets regulations allowed them to sell products from home kitchens, and while this appeared to be an important and valued outlet, there appears to be little additional room for growth. Nonetheless, the returns were higher than for the crafts businesses. The average was $3,328 and the median earnings were $2,616, and the maximum reported earnings was $7,313.

Small but Entrepreneurial

On one level, the food businesses in this category are all alike. Part-time and home-based, these entrepreneurs use their "spare time" and that of other family members to produce the jellies, breads, pies, sweets, noodles and other goods sold at farmers' markets and to individual customers. But, even within the same context and similar set of constraints, some individuals seem to apply innate business skills that put them ahead of the game in terms of earnings. Take for example the case of Becky, whose buying savvy and close recordkeeping seemed to put her ahead of the others in terms of return on labor. Here is how she described the ways she managed to keep her costs low and squeeze more "profit" out of each unit she sold.

Starting a year in advance, Becky and her family pick most of the fruit that she uses from their own land and other open land in the area. She then freezes the fruit to be used throughout the year in production of roughly 1,000 jars of jelly. The other ingredients she needs for her jelly and bread-making she buys in bulk when they go on sale. *"When sugar is on sale at the supermarket, I don't buy five or 10 pounds; I buy 100-200 pounds and store it away. I buy pectin in bulk, not in tiny packages; same with gluten. I buy canning jars when they're on sale at this time of the year; I also scrounge jars, and I give my customers 25 cents for each jar they return to me. They cost 50 cents new."* To leverage the long trip to town, Becky buys her ingredients twice a month when she delivers her bread to 10 regular customers in town.

Following these cost-saving methods and careful calculation of her sales and expenses allows Becky to know that she sells a loaf of bread for $3.25 and only 61 cents of that is the cost of the materials.

Although Laura bakes bread for a bread route and the farmers' market, just as Becky does, costs per bread loaf are significantly more. Laura estimates it costs her $1.75 per loaf in materials. While Laura is able to bake six loaves at a time compared to Becky's five, it takes both of them 1½ hours from grinding to removing the bread from the oven. Although Laura makes more bread to bring to the market each week, Becky's return from the loaves she is baking is significantly higher.

Service businesses included cleaning, child care, lawn care and bookkeeping. These businesses are all one-person operations, and depend on the individual to generate the customers and to deliver the service. All the owners operated these activities part time, fitting them within the constraints of other work activities or household responsibilities. The markets for the cleaning and lawn care businesses are interesting in light of the area's changing demographics: they included seniors who could no longer keep up the maintenance chores in their homes, affluent ranch and resort home owners who sought help with upkeep when in residence, and out-of-state inheritors of properties who were either not yet ready or unable to sell. While these businesses are small, they appear to provide larger returns to the owners than businesses in the previous two sectors. On average, entrepreneurs reported earning $3,378 annually, and the median was $3,000. One individual reported earning $12,350 from her child-care business. On average, the entrepreneurs had $5,170 in assets invested in the businesses; the median was $2,500. The maximum value of reported assets was $15,600 and represented the value of photography equipment. The majority of reported assets in this sector were lawn mowers and photography equipment.

The animal-related businesses included dog breeding, horse training/breaking and animal trapping. There were several home-based breeding operations that, like the food businesses, operated half in and half out of the formal economy. So long as there are fewer than nine litters a year, the breeders can raise home-based puppies and not follow kennel rules, and this is what all the business owners interviewed were doing. At the same time, none of the income was reported. Depending on the number of litters and where they were sold, the sideline could be fairly remunerative.

Catering to a Better Paying Market

Jody and her family stumbled into the dog-breeding business. Originally they bought their first pug because they wanted a dog that would be good with their children. After their first puppy died, they bought an older male and female because the older dogs are cheaper. When their first litter was born, they did a little research on the Internet to see if they could sell the dogs without a license. They learned that as long as they had three or fewer female dogs, they didn't have to be licensed. Next, they talked to their vet about what shots were required to certify a "healthy puppy," and then found out how to register their puppies with the AKC.

They decided to target the "yuppie" market in Denver and placed an ad in the *Denver Post*. They start *"advertising when they're six weeks old. And, nobody can resist a six-week-old dog."* They are contacted by potential buyers either over the phone or via e-mail. They send digital pictures of the dogs to the buyers through e-mail, keeping them updated on the puppies' growth. *"On a weekly basis, I send them an updated — you know, a growth picture ... our first picture is with a coffee cup, so they get an idea of the size of the puppy. So, the puppy's sitting on my kitchen table next to a coffee cup, and they're adorable, I mean, irresistible."*

When the puppies are 10 weeks old, *"we make a trip to Denver and have a central location where ... we meet them (the buyers) all at a central location, deliver the puppies, and then go to Sam's Club and buy groceries."*

They don't sell any of the puppies for less than $500 and make an average of $3,000 a litter. Their costs are quite low both in expenses and labor. As the dogs are small, they consume only about $100 a year in food. They are able to get their entire litter of puppies vet checked for $25. Straight care of the dogs, feeding and cleaning up after them, only takes about 30 minutes a day. They could have up to two litters a year for their three females for an estimated total of $18,000 without being regulated. *"Two litters a year is not too much for a dog to have ... that's their natural cycle ... but they don't live as long."* Since these dogs are Jody's family's pets, they choose to have one litter of puppies a year.

They have considered growing their lucrative operation, but that would mean becoming a regulated kennel. *"To grow any larger, you'd have to have an individual pen for each dog; it has to be heated, and they have to have X amount of square feet for a run. You know, it's pretty much the dog has to be imprisoned in a kennel. And, you have to be inspected quite a bit to maintain that level. So then, that cuts into your profit. When you juggle the numbers, it didn't benefit us to go any larger. Plus, then we would lose ... our big advantage is our puppies are family raised."* In this case, small is manageable, and remunerative enough, for the costs involved.

The horse trainers were men perceived as skilled riders with a talent for domesticating young horses. Generally working alone and around their other work commitments, they earned small amounts of money doing something they loved. The animal trapper, on the other hand, became engaged in his activity opportunistically, finding a ready supply of coyotes near the hog farm on which he worked. Noting that the area had not been hunted for several years, he was able to snare over 100 coyotes the previous season for sale to a fur company that sent buyers across a broad swath of states collecting quality furs. Given the range of reported activities in this group, the range of earnings was also large from a minimum of $1,569, which represented the return to the coyote trapper, to a maximum of $8,342 reported by a dog-breeding entrepreneur. The average annual earnings were $4,677 and the median was $4,950 — the highest reported figures for the four sectors. The reported assets were also higher on average and median, $6,967 and $5,000 respectively. The majority of the assets reported by these entrepreneurs included animal stock and horse training equipment.

Each of these activities, like others in this group of supplementary businesses, has its own built-in limitations to growth that influence both their current size as well as their likely future trajectory. They are:

- *Market constrained:* most serve very small and local markets. Quality influences the capacity of some of them to tap larger or more affluent markets. In others, it has more to do with the lack of vision, or knowledge about how to tap into other opportunities. Glen, for example, notes that he and his partner developed a rope halter that is made *"so good that nobody else [competes with them] and they don't wear out."* Sold to horse sales and feed stores, the market seems to have slowed in his local area, yet marketing is confined to *"just kind of word-of-mouth right now, and they know that we do it, so if they need one, well, they just call us."*
- *Regulation constrained:* allied with the above, safety regulations confine the growth of the food businesses and the dog-breeding businesses. The notion of building a commercial kitchen and addressing other food regulations is daunting to these individuals, and in most instances, doesn't seem to fit with their sense of where they want these activities to go.
- *Production constrained:* there is only so much one individual can do, especially when engaging in high-touch activities like quilting, cake decorating, horse training, cleaning, etc. None of the entrepreneurs interviewed expressed interest in growing their service businesses to a size where employees would be involved. And, one actually expressed aversion based on her previous negative experience in having employees: *"I had nine employees. And … that was not a good experience — I had to hire bookkeepers and all that sort of thing. And, it ended up, I was making no money. I made a lot of money gross, but what I got to spend on groceries was very little."*— Jody
- *Constrained by personal and household responsibilities:* A number of respondents spoke of child-rearing responsibilities or other household responsibilities that

limited the amount of time and attention they could give to the enterprise.[35] What made the activities attractive income supplements was their fit with these primary obligations, and, at the same time, that is what limits their interests in growth. *"Well, it gives me an opportunity to spend more time with my kids, because that's one of the reasons we moved out here. It's really important to me ... I wanted to be able to spend time with them and wanted them to know that they were important to me, that I could take time off and go to a field trip that they were going on or go and read in the classroom. But, I wanted to be able to do something at home, to help prevent me from having to go and get a full-time job."* — Rose

Growth Potential Businesses

Finally, this research identified a few cases in which the individual is using the informal business operation as a testing ground for an idea to take formal if it works out. Six activities fell in this category. They included:

- A photography business in which the owner had just committed to a substantial investment in digital equipment to increase sales in current markets and to capture new markets — photographing horses and other high-quality animals for sales announcements and selling instant photos at rodeo events;
- A beautician doing hair care privately, but preparing to launch a shop;
- A leather crafter who is selling some products in a high-end golf course shop and is moving to Web marketing;
- An animal breeder developing a goat business to sell meat to a growing ethnic market and stock to other breeders; and
- Two baking businesses, where there is potential for growth, but both operated by cautious entrepreneurs not sure they are willing to take the next steps.

What makes these businesses or business owners different from the others? Current earnings give a hint of their potential, on average falling near the top of the range of the figures reported above, around $4,661 a year (median, $4,725). Their investment in assets seems to span a broad range from $150 for one of the bread-baking businesses to $15,600 for the photography business. There seem to be several key ways in which they differ from those among the cluster of businesses discussed above, and in general, they will manifest more than one of the following characteristics.

The owners have tested their markets and have identified a strong interest in their product or service. Pamela, for example, just recently graduated from cosmetology school and has already built up a small clientele through family, friends and acquaintances. Jessica sells eight to 10 pies, and between 18 and 34 dozen

[35]One practitioner and close observer of the microenterprise field in Nebraska noted the family's attitude toward the enterprise was also critical: "It was common to see in ranch/farm relationships where the husband had suffered major financial setbacks in the ranching/farming operation and found it difficult to be positive about the future. They wanted to be supportive of their spouse in their business, but suffered from failure anxiety brought about in their own operations. ... It took a pretty strong person to go it alone until the financial numbers proved that it could work." Rose Jaspersen, e-mail, 26 January 2004. See text on page 45, for more on how supportive family relationships have positioned some informal entrepreneurs for growth.

cinnamon rolls, cookies and runzas (a form of meat and cabbage roll) a week to clients she visits at eight businesses in her town. And, she has received requests for more. Dustin and his wife have been taking school and rodeo photos for some 30 years, and have a steady clientele of parents who seek them out. He's also done some photo shoots for private horse sales, and sees a market there as well. Whether new to the activity or engaged long-term, these entrepreneurs have a good sense that they offer an attractive product or service.

At the same time, *they've recognized a gap in the market that they can fill.* Pamela, again for example, has discovered, with her husband, a community in which hair-cutting services seem to be limited, and where they think there's a natural market. They plan to build a shop on a small property they're in the process of buying. As Pamela said: *"Most people go to North Platte, and that's 30 miles away. The girls in high school would go 30 miles to go tan before prom, cause there isn't a tanning bed in town. ... So, I'm going to get a tanning bed, too. And, there's a lot of older ladies that still don't like to go out of town to go to the salon. They [would] rather stay in their home town ..."* Dustin is investing in new digital equipment to enable him to offer instant photos at rodeos. He also intends to do custom sales photos for owners of prize horses and registered stock, using the capabilities of the equipment to erase extraneous items from the pictures, to enhance the images, and to present the client with instant views of the photos he can purchase. He appears to be on the cutting edge in this respect in his local community and expects the business to thrive, noting that, *"I've got a friend that does this out of Gillette, Wyoming, he does it professionally, so he has been a lot of help to me getting set up to what we need to do, 'cause he's been doing it for years."* Katherine who bakes and decorates cakes for birthdays, weddings and other special occasions notes that there is neither an independent bakery nor one nested in the grocery store of her local community. She reported that the grocery owner *"told me at any time, if you would need anything, you just give me a ring. That, right there, says to me: this guy wants my business — any time. [He is thinking] that he could sell my products."* Each of these entrepreneurs has discovered a niche — from very local to somewhat broader — where the competition seems slim.

Many of these individuals have strong skills and express an entrepreneurial spirit. In this they're not unlike some of the other respondents who also demonstrated an innate business sense in their operations. Here, however, it seems to be combined with a greater willingness to grow and to try new things. The cases of Rose, the goat breeder, and Robin, the leather crafts worker, illustrate how this can lead to bigger things.

A Willingness to Grow

When Rose quit her job and moved with her family to western Nebraska from Colorado, she was faced with either taking a low-paying wage job or finding some way to generate self-employment. Rose explains that it wasn't a hard choice for her. *"With my kids, it makes it real difficult to work for seven dollars an hour, plus pay four dollars an hour for a babysitter, you know, and drive for half an hour each way every day."*

Rejecting a wage job, Rose began to investigate options for self-employment that would allow her to leverage their small 45-acre farm. After doing research, Rose decided to build a meat goat herd. *"Meat goat is one of the fastest growing segments of agriculture right now, and, in Nebraska, it is really way behind. We are probably five or six years behind Oklahoma and Texas in terms of the meat goat market. It's one of those markets that is really up and coming, especially with the fast-growing minorities, like the population anyway of both Muslims and Mexicans and Spanish. They have a real history of using goat meat in their holiday celebrations and that kind of thing, and since we are fairly close to a pretty good market in the Denver metro area, it is something that I was really looking into."*

In order to avoid having to find significant up-front financing for her goat operation, Rose worked out a novel arrangement with a man who raises goats in the central part of the state. *"I use his nannies and then I pay him back in half the kid crop ... I get the nannies. I have to take care of them. I have to give them all their vaccines; feed them; take care of them; take care of the kids. I give him half the kid crop and then at the end of the three years, without having to pay him any extra money, the original nannies will be mine."* With her share of the kids, Rose will build up her own nanny supply and use the proceeds of the kids she sells to invest in additional nannies and goat equipment. This allows her to grow gradually without having to take on additional debt.

Rose intends to grow her nanny herd to 50 head. At that level, she estimates she will be making about $6,000 a year off the sale of the goats for meat and extra nannies to others wishing to build up their own nanny stock. *"That is a significant amount of money in our life. It does not sound like a whole lot, but, for us, that would be a lot."*

Rose doesn't plan to stop there though. Her entrepreneurial spirit shows through in the plethora of ideas she has for leveraging her goat herd once she has it up and running. She'd like to lease out her herd to ranchers, as *"actually, goats will improve a pasture."* This arrangement would mean her goats' feed would be covered and ranchers would provide a fee for the goats' pasture improvement. Additionally, she has investigated producing artisanal cheeses which she believes she could effectively market in the Denver area. Rose believes the meat goat market will grow in Nebraska and hopes to position herself as a supplier of quality goats to others looking to enter the business.

Rose has big plans for her goat herd, but she intends to realistically assess where she is in a few years' time, *"... It is a lot of work and, you know, you want to be able to have something to show for it, I guess. ... in a couple of years, if it's not going to be a money-making proposition, then I'll get out of it, but I really want it to succeed and I want it to work ... 'cause I don't want have to go back to a job."*

Like Rose, Robin was interested in finding self-employment opportunities that would fit in with her other responsibilities: primarily ranch work and childrearing. As her extended family is involved with ranching and rodeos, she decided to try her hand at leather crafts — making chaps, chinks and embellished saddle blankets for use in rodeo or horse shows, as well as child-sized rodeo wear and decorative pillows for the gift market. She does high-quality work and adds touches that set her work off — such as adding a customer's "brand" to the finished item.

She started leather working about seven or eight years ago, but has really started to devote more time to her business in the last few years. In fact, *"it's grown a lot in the last six months. Once you get things operating, it's kind of like wildfire, which is good."* Robin already took steps to expand the reach of her products by placing her pillows and other gift items in the gift shop of a prestigious private golf course in the area. She is paid based on the number of items she sells. This first step to reach a larger market jibes with her overall plan for the business. As she explains, *"Just because here, you're kind of filled up here. We are in a town of 500 people; there is just not a lot to do with that. And, going to craft shows, I don't know, maybe you can make that work, but with the price of gas, to me it is easier for me to stay home, just have a Web site that I can do things from the home. After all, the kids come first."*

Next, Robin plans to leverage her cousin's career in Web design to have him build a Web site for her business. She hopes to attract customers to her products through the Web site *"so you can reach a wider range of people. I think when you get out of this small rural community, there is more money to be spent."*

Finally, *for many of these entrepreneurs, the household conditions either demand or support the ratcheting up of the business.* Dustin and his wife, for example, are a mature, 30-year married couple whose children are grown. They have the time and the interest to build their business. At the same time, the poor cattle returns they had experienced in previous seasons had forced them to sell their cattle and look to other avenues for financial support. The push of ranch economics and the pull of the photo business made it a ripe moment for taking a risk. Jessica, a divorced mother of one, was considering growth less as an opportunity and more as a requirement to sustain her small household. While she still expressed reluctance about what it would take to build a bigger business, her need to be sustainable was pushing her to think about it seriously. Pamela had a husband who supported her ambition to have her own beauty shop. Rose's husband also supported her intent to grow her goat-breeding business, given his own limited income potential. And, Rose felt that the business could be better combined with raising her children than many other options she could consider. Unlike other respondents in this study, these individuals appeared more ready to face the next steps in developing their businesses and consider the implications of formality.

Looking For What?

If there is one image that these microentrepreneurs and informal economy workers convey to outsiders, it is that of rugged individualists, the classic Americans who know how to, and expect to, make a living on their own, with little or no outside help. These Plains people know that they live in a part of the country where the economic engine has to be self-reliance, and where one's own savvy is what will carry you through. So to ask them what type of assistance or support they might want to improve their small-scale economic activities is challenging. Few have considered how additional training or other resources could help develop their businesses. At the same time, the ranching families are already enmeshed in lending arrangements that support their ranching operation. Taking on additional debt for another economic activity doesn't sit well with most of them. Like most Americans, talk for a few minutes about what drives economic choices and the subject of health insurance comes up. It causes people to make job decisions that they might not prefer; it causes others to run risks with their own health or that of their families. It remains an important backdrop to any conversation regarding growing a business. Here is what the respondents said on this and a variety of themes.

Credit

> *"Oh, yeah, a loan would be huge. Who wouldn't like to have some money? To do it really, really well, you know, if I had had the money to start with, initially, and buy 50 nannies and had the money to, you know, I would need the money for fencing. If I could get a loan, a low enough percentage loan, I'd like to do that, too, just to be able to get that money initially and be able to get the fences up because it's going to take a while to build up the herd to where I am getting enough of an income from the herd. It is kind of a thing where you cannot really have that many goats without having the fences up first."*
>
> — Rose

> *"At times I have, yes, but I think, you know what, I am almost kind of scared, because I have never been in a business, never done a business before. I guess I am a little bit hesitant. And, this area is kind of, you know, you gotta see if it is going to work or not."*
>
> —Harriet

Among the entrepreneurs interviewed, there were eight, 28 percent of the sample, who either had experience with credit or would consider taking a loan.

A few of these entrepreneurs had already used credit for their businesses. This included Lisa, a school cafeteria worker, who runs a lawn mowing business catering to absentee owners of family homes and church yards, and who took two consumer loans to purchase lawn mowers for the business. The loans were for $1,500 and $1,000 — for a ride mower, grass catcher and power push mower — for three to four months each with a balloon payment at the end. The interest rate was reported at 4 percent, and the loans were provided by her local community bank. Shirley and her husband had also taken a $5,000 loan to purchase a horse trailer, which they converted into a mobile store for their retail business, selling a wide variety of work gloves at craft shows, rodeos and other venues.

Jody was a third respondent who had lending experience. Unlike many of the others in the sample, Jody had experience running formal businesses as well as generating income informally. Prior to her current businesses (stained glass, dog breeding, a bed and breakfast), she had run two day-care centers, employing nine people. She had borrowed extensively to set up and operate these centers, and reported that *"it ended up, I was making no money. I made a lot of money gross, but what I got to spend on groceries was very little."* Reflecting on how nerve-racking that experience was, she commented: *"That puts a lot of pressure — if you can do your business — you know, if you go pinchers up and you have a big bank loan, that's devastating. If you go pinchers up and you have a room full of stained glass or fabric, oh well, you know, that's just a lesson. But, a bank loan is — that's a lot of stress."*[36] Given the stresses that these entrepreneurs experience due to the uncertainties of ranching, special family needs, and the juggling of economic activities, borrowing money is something that is not lightly done.

Only three others expressed a definite interest in borrowing money. One was Pamela, the beautician, who with her husband planned to purchase a piece of land that would serve as the base for their home and business interests. They expected to borrow some of the required money informally from her grandmother and some formally from the bank. Another was Paul, an occasional caterer, who offered that he would be willing to take credit to build a commercial kitchen to grow his business when he was ready to grow, but that didn't seem like something he'd be doing in the near term. And, the third was Katherine, a baker specializing in cakes, who had a vibrant business and had thought about getting a loan to grow her business more, but questioned *"would you **get** a loan?"* from a bank if she tried.

The majority of the respondents were more like Harriet, risk averse and credit averse. Or, they were ambivalent, willing to consider taking credit at some future point, but not yet certain that this was the right course. And, there were a variety of reasons why credit did not make sense for them and their businesses.

For some, the business is still too new and too small. Without further testing of the market, the entrepreneurs feel that they could get way ahead of themselves, having to convert all their earnings into loan repayments without necessarily increasing their market share overall. Even those with some good experience hesitate to "raise the ante" on their operations. Becky, for example, one of the

[36]When asked what pinchers up meant, Jody answered, *"Oh. When a crab dies, it falls on its back, and its little pinchers go [up]."*

savviest food producers in the sample, questioned the wisdom of investing in a commercial kitchen to increase her market for the jams and pies she made. *"Well, I've thought about it,"* she noted, but she'd have to first understand all the requirements associated with building and maintaining a certified kitchen, and then she'd need to figure out how long it would take her to pay it off because *"everything I made would go to paying off the kitchen until that was done."* Because the money she makes from her farmers' markets sales covers the grocery bill for the family all summer long, that seemed to be a powerful brake on any upgrading of the business.

Even Robin, the leather crafter, who had developed an interesting product line and was poised to test market expansion through Internet sales, was reluctant. She said that while a loan might enable her to purchase higher quality sewing machines, *"I don't know that I would, no. It is just something ... I enjoy doing it, but I don't know that I would want to take out a large loan just to get this going. I would rather wait a few years and hopefully have the money and just do it that way."* This way of growing the business, building one's own cash reserves and then investing, appealed not only to her, but also to others. That was how Dustin was able to purchase his advanced camera equipment, how Glen purchased all his horse-riding gear, and how Robert gathered together his carpentry equipment. This strategy of slow accumulation of the tools of the trade is a common approach of microentrepreneurs.

Many of the other businesses are not resource-intensive, or use assets purchased for other purposes. Patty, for example, reported that there was little need for credit for her home cleaning business: *"You don't need to borrow money to make money — not in a situation like this anyway."* Of course, she had a personal car that she used, and required her customers to provide their own vacuums and cleaning supplies. In this way, she was unlike many of the urban informal microentrepreneurs interviewed for an earlier study, who had few household assets to draw upon, and could foresee a rapid return to some financial investments.[37] Others whose businesses run on few external resources include the home-based dog breeders, the sewers and quilters, and the day-care and pre-school businesses.

Business Skills

Is there anything else you need to learn ... that would advance this particular economic activity ...?

> *"Possibly a little more about marketing. How to market the product, possibly ... I did check into a couple of ... at the mall, there is a store called GNC, and I had gone up there and visited with the man about possibly bringing my bread in their store and selling it like that, but it changed hands and then I never followed up."*
>
> — Laura

[37]See Edgcomb and Armington, pages 35-36 for a discussion of the investments Latino entrepreneurs had made in their cleaning businesses. In addition, a couple of the entrepreneurs also saw the opportunity to grow these businesses through the purchase of floor strippers and polishers, seeing an additional strong market for businesses that could clean and polish floors in corporate offices and local businesses.

Do you think taking a business class would be helpful?

I think taking a business class probably would help ... And, I think time gets away from me; our last one, she is in her fifth year [of] college right now, so she's been out of the house going on five years now. I had plenty of time to contemplate this, and I just haven't done it yet."

— Julie

There is a greater interest in learning business skills than in accessing credit. At the same time, however, more respondents than not express that interest conceptually rather than as a near-term objective. There's a tension between what they clearly acknowledge they need to learn and the obstacles they see in the way of acting on the need.

The most identified deficiencies that entrepreneurs describe in themselves relate to pricing, marketing and managing their accounts. Pricing is always challenging: there's the question of how much does the product or service actually cost, and then there's the question as to whether the customer will actually pay what it's worth. There's a lot of refusal to face the actual labor costs associated with productive activities. When these entrepreneurs are asked to relate their costs to their earnings, many refuse to even reflect on the hours they spend per item. When asked about the time she spends on her bread and jelly-making, Becky said she doesn't want to count her own labor because *"then I won't be making anything."*

In addition, many express the real concern that even if they could determine a price that would provide them a fair return to labor, they would have difficulty finding a market on those terms. Several note real price resistance among their customers. *"Most people can go to Wal-Mart or whatever and buy a $3 frame and most of them are presentable. They don't last as good. ..."* — Dustin

Others know what they need to do, but haven't yet had the heart to do it. As Julie, a seamstress who does alterations as well as creates bridal party gowns from scratch, says:

"Probably what I need to do is even for friends; what I need to do is just start saying: 'I charge $8 an hour and possibly to make a dress is going to take me four or five hours. So, one dress is going possibly to cost you anywhere from $24 or $32 to $40.' So, they know right upfront. And then, if I'm making seven dresses, the smaller bridesmaids' dresses, sometimes they are quicker, because just they have not much details. But, so they know. And, if I give them a bill for $200 or something, they are not surprised, they are not shocked."

Learning how to sell one's fair price is not an easily mastered skill.

Many respondents recognize that their financial skills are also wanting, and see that a solution could be in learning or refreshing their bookkeeping skills as well as mastering computer-based programs that would make managing their revenues and expenses easier. Rose, the goat breeder, comments: *"that would be a very good help, just so that I could get things lined out, so I can take a look, print out a sheet, and say, 'Okay, this is how much money I am spending on this and this is where we are coming out at the end of the year,' and take a look at this area to see if we can cut down somehow on expenses and increase our profit margin."*

But, whether they will ever take the initiative to develop these skills is another matter indeed. Like Julie, some view the possibility of business skills training like a visit to the dentist — necessary, but not something that makes it to the top of the to-do list. Pamela, the beautician about to open a shop, expresses the tension well. She frankly says that *"... I'm nervous about learning how to run the whole business thing, the taxes, and insurance on the place, and all that kind of stuff."* And, she's aware of a business course that could introduce her to the information and skills she might need. Yet, she says, *"my husband can't go to it with me, and the only time we can do it will be in the summer, and I don't know, I think I'm going to wing it. We have friends ... they have a business and they said they would help."*[38] Others are not aware of any business skills training available in the area, and express their concern that anything that might be available would be inconvenient in terms of time and place. While these rural Nebraskans are used to driving long distances to get where they want and need to go, they also husband their time carefully and fear committing to something that might be long term and taxing.

And, despite the fact that distance-learning is becoming common in the small schools that dot these towns, no one has thought to seek business information on the Internet, again perhaps, because it seems too hard to find. Jody, the stained-glass maker, for example, says that *"... I don't know where to look. I mean, in between everything else I do, I haven't sat down and — I know that it is out there. But, as far as for it to slap me in the face, it has not ... And, to my knowledge, to me ... looking on Google, I don't think there's a Web site, go girl, get this information type thing. ... You know what I mean? It would take me three hours to sit there and look it up and go here, there and everywhere, and that, I don't have that kind of time."* Asked if she would use a Web resource if she could find it, however, she replies, *"Oh, I would, yeah. Because, you know, there's probably a way."*

Busy people as they are, if they're to seek any business information or skills training, access needs to be easy, and the information must address their specific information need in as short a time as possible to get the job done.

Industry-based Skills

Do you need any additional training or information or education?

"No, I have my Time/Life books."

— Robert

[38]The University of Nebraska's Nebraska EDGE (Enhancing, Developing and Growing Entrepreneurs) program is an economic and community development strategy for all Nebraska communities. EDGE provides comprehensive training and technical assistance for start-up and existing businesses. To accomplish the goal of providing quality services, EDGE contracts with business consultants and area business leaders to provide training and technical assistance, and depends on local partners, such as local banks, utility companies, chambers of commerce and economic development organizations to provide networks and infrastructure. Over the last 10 years, the EDGE program has assisted nearly 2,000 emerging and existing business owners through the completion of a marketing and financial management plan for their businesses. The EDGE program offers two courses aimed at small businesses. One class — "Business Start-ups" — is geared toward individuals that have an idea for a business but have not yet set their idea in motion. This course meets once a week for 10 weeks, and helps individuals think through crucial questions before starting their businesses. "Entrepreneurs" is intended for those looking to expand their existing businesses and involves developing a comprehensive business plan. This class is 12 sessions long and takes place over 12 to 15 weeks. The courses are offered in 10 to 12 communities annually throughout the state.

"If it was convenient, I would take some training on it, yes. Here, it is kind of hard to find. It would be, I guess, probably, the operating of the computer side of it; you can always learn something there, I think, or even the photography side, just on the horse photography, equine photography."

— Dustin

When asked if they need more training on their craft or in their industry, only a few entrepreneurs said that they do. Several, like Dustin, feel that there are computer-based technologies that would improve what they're doing and that they would find helpful to learn. They include Harriet, the graphics printer, and Judith, who's doing manual bookkeeping for her trucker client.

Others, like Jessica, the baker, and Julie, the seamstress, acknowledge that there's certainly more to learn about their trades. At the same time, however, there's a sense conveyed that this additional training, while it might be desirable or enjoyable to learn, may not really be necessary in the markets they're serving. Lisa, the lawn mower, for example, expressed an interest in learning landscaping, but said that her clientele didn't really need those services: *"You know, if I was really serious and wanted to go on and move to a bigger town and grow and be able to expand, yeah, that would be a consideration. But, just now, here in town, I would probably never do that."* Julie also reports that *"the class that I would love, that I maybe really would like to take, would be some kind of alteration class, because everybody is satisfied with what I do, but I wouldn't mind taking an alteration class. ... That would be interesting."* So while the intrinsic interest might be there, the motivation for advancing in one's craft doesn't seem a powerful one for many. Without the drive to access larger markets, and with that a need to keep up with the competition, the push to seek out new information is limited.

Insurance

"I worked the weekend shift down at the distribution center, because there were the benefits — the insurance, the health insurance — because when you have your own private [insurance], when you ranch, you have to have health insurance, just because if you don't, you don't know whether you are going to be able to survive or not. Because if you ever have to have [it] and our youngest daughter she had scoliosis surgery two years ago in September and you just don't know."

— Kate

What is the hardest part or what are some of the drawbacks to working informally in this way?

"Well, like I said, probably not having health insurance is probably the biggest thing, because it is just too, it is prohibitively expensive to buy it on your own. If you have a job that provides it, you can afford it."

— Ed

A constant refrain in the interviews is the struggle to get, maintain and pay for health insurance. Ranchers as owner-operators of their agricultural business must secure their own health insurance. And, the costs to finance a family's care are high. Some have bitten the bullet and paid for coverage. Others have taken a riskier strategy, forgoing insurance for themselves while having their children covered through state-managed Medicaid programs. One of these is Patty. After quitting her job, Patty lost her health insurance, such as it was. She explains that now that she's self-employed she *"can't afford it."* However, in the short-term, not having insurance has actually helped her family's bottom line, because their prescriptions and co-pays were so expensive under their health insurance plan. Further, she reports: *"I could not believe it, but I went and had prescriptions filled and they were cheaper ... the pills and doctors' visits have gotten cheaper, because I didn't have insurance. I couldn't believe it."* Unfortunately if she encounters any major medical expenses, she may miss her insurance more than she does now.

Still others have been lucky enough to obtain jobs that offer health benefits, and the respondents are clear about how important those benefits are in making the decision to pursue employment. As Shirley says, *"Yeah, but my biggest thing is health insurance is so expensive nowadays, and you've got to do anything you can to make more money."* It is what has propelled some to work at the Wal-Mart distribution center even though this requires long-distance driving and long hours away from home. It is what has motivated others to new positions at the county roads departments even though their true passion is ranch work. And, for those who can't get those jobs, the worries about health insurance are ever present.

FORMALIZATION

> *"... you know, I am trying to, you know, keep track of my records and my paperwork and make sure that this is worth the work that I put into it. I realize, if it keeps growing that, honesty is on the line, you have to report your income, so ..."*
>
> — Jessica

> *"This photography business, we declared quite a little of it, because we have quite a lot of expense involved. A lot of the cash we don't turn in. A lot of the rodeo pictures will be cash."*
>
> — Dustin

As discussed earlier in this study, these rural entrepreneurs approach the issue of formalization in a variety of ways, and they can be placed in a hierarchy according to their level of compliance with (or interest in complying with) the requirements of legal registration, adherence to regulations and taxation policies.

TABLE 4: CURRENT BUSINESS STATUS

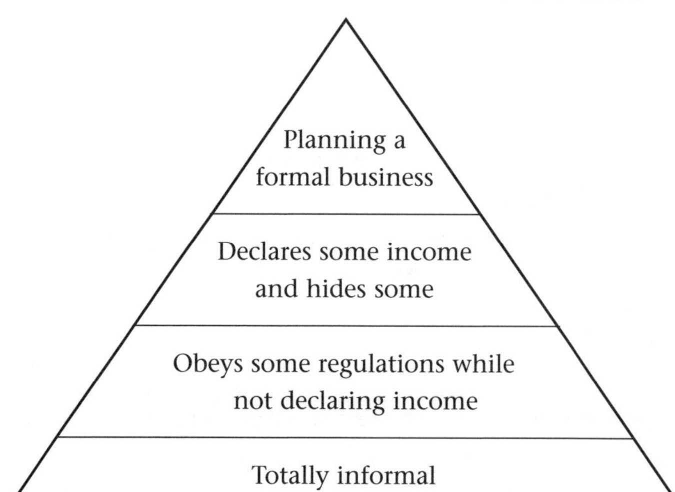

The largest group of entrepreneurs, some 72 percent, operated at least one business in a totally informal manner. The businesses are not legally registered; the owners do not declare any earnings, nor do they follow any regulations associated with the industry in which they operate. The businesses include house cleaning; child care; the sewing, quilting, leather and wood crafts; and the horse-breaking, tack-making and selling businesses.

Twenty-eight percent of the entrepreneurs operate at least one business in which they follow some of the "rules of the game." Largely this includes the women food producers who conform to the labeling and public disclosure requirements that permit them to sell at farmers' markets. It also includes the dog breeders who follow the regulations with respect to home-based pet raising, and a small mobile retail business (selling work gloves at rodeos and craft shows) that pays sales tax on its sales. What none of them do, however, is declare any of the revenue from that business on their personal income tax.

Three entrepreneurs, or 10 percent of the sample, have a formally recognized business on which they declare part of the income. They include a photographer, a horse trainer and a carpenter who treat their revenues differently depending on the amount of money involved, the source, or the type of transaction (cash or check). During the course of this study, the researchers met other business owners who also applied this approach to their business, often declaring a majority of the revenues, but pocketing some amounts for household or personal use.

Finally, one entrepreneur, representing just 3 percent of the sample, was ready to take all the steps necessary to formalize her business. That was Pamela who was on the verge of opening the beauty salon after nine months of testing her business informally.

But, while she was the only one who was quite near to formalizing, there were others like Jessica who expressed a cautious but open attitude towards moving to a more visible, registered and regulated business. Including her, there were at least nine, or 31 percent of the group, who were considering the idea to one degree or another. Among them were two bakers, three crafters, one graphics printer, a husband and wife retail team focused on selling work gloves, a housecleaner, and Jessica, one of the bakers. She and Patty, a relatively new housecleaner, were the closest to making the transition. Both were keeping some form of financial records, and were willing to report their income as their businesses grew. Patty especially noted the importance of keeping track, because she thought her business would grow substantially over the next year and wanted to be sure that she both covered her direct costs, paid into Social Security, and earned a living:

> *"... I have to fill out all these papers and get all this stuff wrote down. Like, I'll see my attorney and I haven't got that done. I just got it in a little notebook now, what I've made and where I've been and stuff. But, I need to get it wrote out and get it filled out so I can go and talk to him about it, and then, I'll know month-for-month where I'm at and week-to-week and stuff like that."*

But, making the leap isn't always that easy. The calculation of what will be lost and what will be gained is hard to make. And, that calculation isn't always just in terms of the dollars and cents of lost income to taxes. It has a lot to do with the implications of taking a business out of the home and putting it on the street, or of increasing the level of effort involved, or dealing with the complications that regulatory and tax compliance might bring. Katherine, a successful cake maker, exemplifies how much thought goes into making the transition.

Cake Shop Dreams

Although she swore she never would, Katherine has become quite a baker. After receiving professional training and working in a grocery store bakery for two years, she decided to branch out on her own and start a cake-baking business that would fit around her other wage-earning activities. Now, she enjoys baking, citing the *"learning, being around people … kind of a little adventure"* as primary reasons for her satisfaction.

At this point, she handles cake orders for both large events, like weddings and other special parties, and small recurring events, such as Mother's Day, birthdays and graduation. During a busy month with a big event, *"You could easily make $500 a month."* When she bakes a 9-by-13 cake, for which she charges $20, *"I figured the most that it could possibly cost me, and I think it would be on the outside, would be $4."*

The steady demand for her product and satisfied customers — *"It's growing … and they are satisfied. I never had a return or rejection of any kind,"* — have led Katherine to dream of opening a cake and floral shop. This decision is not an easy one for her however. She feels strongly that she would need to be at her business full time to make it successful. *"The thing I've seen in this area is, you've got to be there, you have to have a door open. I have seen too many … closed and they think it is at their convenience. You cannot really run a place like that."*

Katherine also feels there may be difficulties finding a suitable building and bringing it up to code for a cake shop. She frets about the money involved in this effort, but also feels much of the work she could do herself. *"I think that is probably the biggest thing what is stopping me right now, just the building … and enough money to start on your own. I don't know what it would take to start it. I have the stuff out of my home and I don't think it would take that much … A person could do a lot of this stuff yourself, like building counters or …"* So, Katherine sits, debating the pros and cons, trying to build her business up bit-by-bit and putting off the big decision of opening a permanent cake shop.

Where to Go From Here?

"It is kind of a little adventure. I see a lot of products all the time, so I could see, you know, oh, I could do that. After you have done this so long, it is kind of like an addiction and you can do that. It is a gratification."
— Katherine

"I love the variety ... I love the independence."
— Robert

"I just love making people feel good about themselves. You give them a new good haircut, and it makes them feel good. That's probably the thing I love the most about it, making people feel good."
— Pamela

"For me it's also creativity, I really do enjoy making something out of nothing."
— Marilyn

Much of the previous pages has focused on the characteristics of the small-scale economic activities of these informal entrepreneurs, how they fit into very complex household economic portfolios, and the constraints and opportunities they present for further growth. But, it would be wrong if this analysis did not try to convey the passion these individuals feel about their work. More than a job, more than just another way to make money, for many of these respondents, the microenterprise offers a way to exercise creativity and autonomy, to produce products or offer services that are admired by others and offer pleasure. No one in the study spoke of his or her job at Wal-Mart or at the roads departments, or in the school systems, or in the motel on the highway with any of the same spirit or enthusiasm.

This is not a new finding. Repeatedly interviews with microentrepreneurs generate the same spontaneous expressions of satisfaction in their work. In a world where most entry-level and bottom-rung positions offer little opportunity for independent decisionmaking, flexibility, problem-solving and control over one's environment, a small sideline provides an arena where those qualities can be experienced.[39] In rural Nebraska, of course, it is less a choice between formal employment and self-employment than a scramble to generate as many income streams as possible given the dearth of employment alternatives. But, to think that

[39]There is no more powerful expression of what low-wage workers normally experience than that presented in Barbara Ehrenreich, *Nickel and Dimed: On (Not) Getting By in America* (New York: Henry Holt and Company, 2001). Reading the book helps one understand the persistence with which workers will seek to break out of these bonds through self-employment, even if that piece can only provide a partial income to the household.

this is the whole of it would be a mistake. People also create these businesses for the sense of purpose they gain from them and their intrinsic rewards.

> *"And, you know, somebody said, 'Why do you do that?' And, I said, 'Well, instead of going somewhere on weekends for vacation, I guess we'll just go home to the country and then work, and that's almost as relaxing and as much fun as going on vacation anyway, you know?' I mean, we just like that lifestyle of being by ourselves and working the cattle and land."*
>
> — Tara

> *"Our ideal dream is both to just stay at home and ranch, but, unfortunately, things don't meet, so we've had to spread ourselves and do a lot of different things to make it work. It is important that the kids are raised in the country. ..."*
>
> — Robin

> *"This is a great place to raise kids."*
>
> — Pete

> *"No, it's, we like living out in the country, we like the atmosphere ... the noise we create is our own, you know, you can hear the animals and see the stars and it is a great place to raise kids and I would not change that for the world. And, there are, I suppose material things that you give up; that's a small price to pay though."*
>
> — Penny

The second important point to emphasize is the hold that rural Nebraska has on those who were interviewed in this study. Despite the hardships, despite the anxieties that are part and parcel of modern small-scale ranching, the respondents represent the population that doesn't want to leave. These are the people who will be the last to give up their landholdings or their stake in local communities. They are willing to do whatever it takes to keep themselves here. And, as this study shows, that takes "quite a little."[40] Whether their children will stay (or return in the case of college-aged sons and daughters) is another matter. Respondents spoke of adult children who had moved to Lincoln for school and stayed, and others who had moved to the larger cities in western Nebraska in pursuit of work. Those with ranch holdings, of course, will be the ones most likely to try to keep family around. How successful they'll be will depend on cattle's future prospects and the fruitfulness of their other ventures. And that, in turn, may depend on their ability to take their enterprises to another level. Those interested in helping them succeed need to look at how both governmental policies and microenterprise program practices might be designed to better help them on the way.

Policy

A consideration of policies to assist informal rural entrepreneurs clearly intersects with larger policy considerations with respect to preserving rural life and livelihoods

[40] "Quite a little," meaning a lot was a common expression used by the respondents.

across the United States. And, as the first chapter of this study indicated, their preservation in the Great Plains states is today clouded in doubt. There are some who think that the population decline is inevitable and not necessarily unwelcome. Nicholas D. Kristof, columnist for the *New York Times* calls the small depopulating towns of the area "a reminder that the oversettlement of the Great Plains has turned out to be a 150-year-long mistake, one of the longest–running and most costly errors in American history."[41] Geographers Frank and Deborah Popper have noted that the Great Plains is an area that has already suffered through two boom and bust cycles, and is now likely in a third.[42] They proposed a concept called "the Buffalo Commons" in response, a vision suggesting that the Plains future is a return to its prairie existence, hosting buffalo, prairie dogs and other creatures, and where lands that were abandoned or "not working well either environmentally or economically" would be restored and returned to lighter uses that "fall between intensive cultivation/extraction and pure wilderness."[43] This notion, first proposed in 1987, has been debated, discussed, challenged and supported over the years. And, in fact, on some levels, the Commons is being created through a combination of public policies[44] and private initiatives[45] that have led to the re-establishment of buffalo herds and a consolidation of lands in several of the states. This approach acknowledges the population losses, yet offers a place for the smaller number who remain either as stewards of these lands and herds, or workers in a tourist industry that would emerge as the Buffalo Commons captures the imagination of the U.S. tourist.

There are other visions for the salvation of the region. Sustainable ranching is one that complements the Commons vision — ranching that depends on grass more than grain, uses fewer antibiotics, skips the feedlot, is less resource-intensive, and focused on producing a higher-quality meat for higher-end markets. Another complement is agricultural tourism. But, there are those who still seek answers in industry, though with limited results. *The New York Times* reports that "hundreds of counties" across the Great Plains have created industrial parks and built buildings

[41]"Making Way for Buffalo," *New York Times,* 29 October 2003, A25.

[42]According to the Poppers, "The first began with the 1862 Homestead Act that gave a pioneer family 160 acres of free federal land if it could farm it for five years. The cycle reached its zenith in the atypical heavy-rain years of the 1870s. Its nadir hit in the 1890s with widespread starvation and large convoys of fully loaded wagon trains headed east, out of the Plains. The second upswing began in the early 1900s with new homesteading laws that allowed settlers up to 640 acres of free federal land. It reached its height during World War I when American wheat replaced European production lost to the battlefields. It bottomed in the 1930s with the Great Depression, drought, the Dust Bowl, the abolition of homesteading, and John Steinbeck's *Grapes of Wrath* Okies driving, hitchhiking or rail-hopping west to California. As a cumulative result of the two cycles, many deep-rural Plains towns and counties had their largest populations in 1930 or 1920 or even 1890 and have declined steadily ever since." The authors go on to note that the Plains may be in the bust phase of a third cycle that had its boom period from the 1940s to 1970s, which "featured first the introduction of large-scale federal agricultural subsidies and then energy-development ones. But, the mid-1980s found large parts of the Plains' farm, ranch, energy and mining economies in near-depression as the national economy, federal policies and global markets shifted. Population losses had accelerated; young people in particular had left. Soil erosion approached Dust Bowl-era rates. The Ogallala Aquifer, the source of agricultural and urban groundwater for much of the southern two-thirds of the Plains, was dropping fast. The Interior Department's Bureau of Reclamation no longer built the big dam and irrigation projects that underwrote large chunks of Plains economic development." *The Buffalo Commons as Regional Metaphor and Geographic Method,* undated, available from http://www.gprc.org/buffalo_commons_popper.html; Internet.

[43]Frank and Deborah Popper, *The Buffalo Commons as Regional Metaphor.*

[44]As examples, Frank and Deborah Popper cite that the Plains Indians have created a consortium of 44 governments to reinvigorate buffalo production; the state of North Dakota has revised its policies to make loans available to buffalo ranchers and offers other services to them. Montana State University has a Center for Bison Studies.

[45]Ted Turner has created substantial buffalo ranches in Nebraska and Montana to produce bison meat for a new chain of restaurants, Ted's Montana Grill, he has launched. "Bison Burgers, for Humanity's Sake," *New York Times,* 5 October, 2003, III: 1.

on speculation hoping to attract new industries and jobs, "and their industrial parks and new buildings sit empty."[46]

The fate of the Great Plains is dramatic, but it is not the only rural area in the United States facing severe economic challenges. The Poppers cite the lower Mississippi Delta, central Appalachia, northern New England, and the Pacific Northwest. "West Virginia coal, Minnesota iron, Illinois and Louisiana farm, and Michigan automobile towns and their surrounding areas have recorded serious population and economic losses, as shown by their gap-toothed blocks and deserted buildings, whether empty storefronts, car dealerships, barns, breakers or factories. Such places often experience environmental degradation as well. ..."[47]

In the face of these challenges, looking to locally grown entrepreneurship as part of the solution is just common sense. Whether one accepts that a Buffalo Commons future, and a smaller population base, is the fate of the Plains, or whether one thinks that depopulation can be fought via governmental support and intervention via a New Homestead Act,[48] all the jobs needed are not going to come from the outside, and people will continue to try to grow their own. In a world of economic uncertainty there need to be fall-back positions for the rural residents who remain. This is not unrecognized at the state level. The National Governors Association Center for Best Practices endorses support for "entrepreneurship outside the agricultural sector" as one of three key economic development strategies for rural states.[49] And, the State of Nebraska has been a supporter of microenterprise development for some time, channeling funds through the Nebraska Microenterprise Partnership Fund for re-lending and re-granting to microenterprise organizations, across the state, that have demonstrated strong capacity to deliver a range of important services to microentrepreneurs.[50] The questions are whether current levels of investment are sufficient to make a difference, and whether there need to be some broader "enabling" initiatives that can support the work done by microenterprise service providers.

Funding

Out of 13 grantees of the Nebraska Microenterprise Partnership Fund, seven provide services in the 51 rural counties of the state. Their staffing is limited to 13 individuals offering direct services in these areas. The Rural Enterprise Assistance Project (REAP) of the Center for Rural Affairs, the largest microenterprise presence in the rural counties, in particular, has one loan officer/technical assistance provider per

---

[46] "Amid Dying Plains Towns, One Makes a Last Stand for New Jobs and People," New York Times, 1 December 2003, A:1, 18.

[47] Frank and Deborah Popper.

[48] The New Homestead Act offers action to reverse rural community decline, including support for asset building and microenterprise development. It offers incentives to reside in and establish businesses in counties that have lost at least 10 percent of their population over the last 20 years. To assist individuals, the bill offers forgiveness on college loans, a tax credit for home purchases, home value protection and individual homestead accounts to help build savings and access to credit for people in high out-migration areas. Business assistance includes tax credits, accelerated equipment depreciation and a $3-billion venture capital fund for business development in high out-migration areas.

[49] The other two are supporting "clusters of interconnected businesses" with academic, financial and other resources and supporting "diversification and value-added agriculture practices." See *Innovative State Policy Options to Promote Rural Economic Development,* Issue Brief, February 2003, 1.

[50] The Nebraska Microenterprise Partnership Fund (NMPF) is a statewide financial intermediary dedicated to supporting microenterprise practitioners, drawing financial support from various national- and state-level sources and then awarding grants, loans and related products to microenterprise programs through an annual "request for proposal" process.

16 counties on average. The EDGE program has 1.5 paid staff to coordinate the services of approximately 35 outside providers offering training, technical assistance and linkages to local bank capital to both rural and urban counties. Grow Nebraska, which provides marketing services and technical assistance for specialty food producers and crafters, has a staff of 3.5 and an annual budget of $250,000 to serve the whole state. During Fiscal Year 2003, the Nebraska Microenterprise Partnership Fund reports 66 individuals receiving training and technical assistance in the seven counties that are the subject of this research. One loan was disbursed in the same seven counties.

Despite the efforts of these programs, the majority of the respondents had never heard of any of them or others that might potentially be of use. While this may suggest something about the need for better marketing by these organizations, it probably says more about how thinly stretched they are in their efforts to serve these areas. Additional financial support is required to achieve deeper coverage of the rural counties and to refine strategies to reach out to more of these informal entrepreneurs.

In alliance with microenterprise service providers, policymakers might consider other strategies to promote the capacity of individuals to grow their enterprises. The New Homestead Act proposes financial incentives, such as tax credits for owner-operated businesses with five or fewer employees (equal to 30 percent of the investment in starting or expanding a microenterprise — up to a lifetime maximum of $25,000) and Individual Homestead Accounts (a form of Individual Development Account) for investments in businesses, first-time home purchases, and un-reimbursed medical expenses. This type of support might stimulate some of the entrepreneurs who are cautiously considering expanding their enterprises to look at the option more seriously. And, while one doesn't want to encourage ill-conceived ventures, there are individuals who, with technical assistance, might successfully make the transition to a growing formal business.

It is also interesting to note that in the course of this study, the researchers interviewed 13 additional informal economy participants whose income crossed the low-income threshold, but whose better economic position was equally based on income patching and an array of business activities. Among this group were an entrepreneur who developed and sold a new type of portable fencing, a crafter with a unique feather-based line of decorative products, a quilter, a photographer and a leatherworker. There were also individuals with struggling formal businesses, including a monogramming operation and a hardware store. The push towards entrepreneurial activity is pervasive throughout the low- to moderate-income population, and for many is what keeps them above the low-income line.[51]

The approach embodied in the New Homestead Act would cover all these individuals. It is similar in spirit to proposals made by informal economy researchers who, having found much to admire in "informal economies of growth," such as central Italy, Cuban Miami and Hong Kong, believe that these patterns can be replicated where state and local governments cooperate in providing tax

[51]The Nebraska Microenterprise Partnership Fund is engaged in exploratory research regarding what they perceive to be a financing gap (that is, the availability of loans between $25,000 and $150,000) for businesses as they grow. Not only financing of this size, but also appropriate technical assistance services would be valuable to individuals like these 13.

incentives, funding for business development services, and other supports. Certainly a geographically dispersed area like rural Nebraska presents more considerable challenges than an urban setting, but the region also reflects strengths — physical and human — that offer a foundation for further entrepreneurial growth.[52]

Taxation, Business Licensing and Regulation

By definition, informal entrepreneurs do not operate in full compliance with applicable laws and regulations regarding taxation, incorporation, registration, licensing, health and safety codes, and others. In western Nebraska, this research uncovered some individuals who operated totally outside all the rules and regulations, and others who respected some of the "rules of the game," while ignoring others. Examples included the food producers who met the requirements to sell at the farmers' markets and the dog breeders who adhered to the limits on home-based breeding. One of the fears expressed by these entrepreneurs was encroaching taxation and regulation. The carpenter, worried about charging sales tax on his work, and the food producers, worried that the regulations for participating in farmers' markets would tighten, represent the face of those who fear that they won't be able to meet the new requirements.

It is beyond the scope of this research to assess the value or need for specific changes in these and other policies. But, what must be recognized is that the impact on livelihoods can be significant. Two questions need to be asked: Is this change necessary? And, if it is, how can it be introduced in a way that enables people to successfully meet the regulation, rather than lose their opportunity to earn revenue?

Practice

In addition to policy issues, this study raises a set of issues for microenterprise development programs to consider. Certainly, most experienced rural program practitioners would not be surprised by the range of informal work described here, as well as the range of perspectives that these informal economy participants bring to their endeavors. In summary, the sector contains:

- Informal workers who sell or barter their labor sometimes regularly, sometimes seasonally and sometimes erratically. They work for neighbors, for local ranchers and other businesses. Their work is not a subject for microenterprise assistance.
- Informal entrepreneurs who see their enterprise as a sideline that provides both household income and personal satisfaction, but which will always likely stay small and supplementary to other sources of income in the household.
- Informal entrepreneurs who are interested in growing their enterprise or are cautiously considering it. They are the ones who may transition their

[52]For more on proposals for supporting regional informal economies, see Alejandro Portes, Manuel Castells and Lauren A. Benton, "Conclusion: the Policy Implications of Informality," *The Informal Economy: Studies in Advanced and Less Developed Countries,* eds. Alejandro Portes, Manuel Castells and Lauren A. Benton (Baltimore: Johns Hopkins University Press, 1989), 306-307.

economic activities to more formal status as they pursue growth. Earlier, six of the group (21 percent) were characterized as presenting growth potential and nine (31 percent) appeared as potentially interested in moving towards more formal operations.

The group also contained at least three entrepreneurs who described "dream businesses," enterprises that would take what they were doing and move it to a higher level. For Jody, it was a bed and breakfast on her ranch through which she could reach the agri-tourism market, offering people the opportunity to live and work on her family's ranch and to whom she could sell her breads and jellies, and other items. For Marilyn, it was opening a shop that sold crafts and antiques; Katherine had a similar idea, but in her case, it combined a bakery and floral shop in one. To what extent are these feasible dreams? It is not clear, but each could benefit from guidance in assessing the venture, and help in planning it if the indications are right.

But, if microenterprise development programs are interested in reaching a Jody, a Marilyn, or a Katherine, there may need to be an adjustment in the services provided. Over and over, respondents mentioned their lack of time to commit to a long-term training activity, or the distances or family obligations that create barriers to participation. And, some who had heard of the EDGE class, had been reluctant to enroll. Still others had no awareness of the existence of entrepreneurial services, despite current program promotions.

These realities — and others discussed in this report — suggest that programs may need to consider new avenues to serve this population. This is said with real acknowledgment of all the efforts that Nebraskan microenterprise programs have made to reach out across the state, and the real cost issues involved in attempting to do more. Experienced program practitioners note that it is not financially feasible to reach out to every informal entrepreneur in the state, and that it is, therefore, incumbent upon programs to direct their resources to those who are ready to take advantage of program services. This means that programs have had to design a "front door" to informal entrepreneurs that is inviting, but that at the same time, requires these entrepreneurs to take specific actions to demonstrate their readiness to use program resources wisely. For REAP, for example, this historically involved a series of steps from, first, attending an introductory meeting to, second, entering an orientation training, to joining a group, and then, contributing to a loan-loss reserve. For EDGE, the "front door" involved up-front marketing of the possibility of a training program, if enough people either paid or raised tuition to make it happen. In each instance, there was an explicit set of decisions made regarding how best to reach out to informal entrepreneurs and under what conditions.[53]

All this makes sense. The question is: What else might be done to go a little deeper? To reach out a little further to the 10 to 30 percent standing a little farther away from the front door? The following suggestions are offered in that light.

[53]Thanks to Eugene Severans for this metaphor and explanation of the "front door," e-mail, 26 January 2004.

Marketing and Promotion

No matter how hard microenterprise programs have tried to get the word out, there remain large numbers of people who don't know that these programs exist. Marketing remains a critical issue and needs to be approached in a variety of ways.[54] Part of the issue may lie in the message itself. A number of the respondents in this study would not describe their activity as a business. To them it is just one more sideline to make a little money. If that is how they think about their endeavors, messages that promote formal business planning or business credit may not reach their ears. Microenterprise programs need to promote and market the notion of entrepreneurship as much as the services themselves. Rural informal entrepreneurs need to see what they do in a new light, and understand that:

- What they do makes a vital contribution to the economic health not only of their households, but also of the communities in which they reside. Their work is as essential to the future of their region as any Wal-Mart that may arrive upon the scene.
- What they are engaged in are businesses, or activities that can become viable businesses, if they learn and apply a set of business concepts to their operation. While some of this may not be easy, these concepts can be mastered and can make a difference in the returns they achieve from their work.[55]

This recasting of what they do can make them receptive to services that they would not consider before. But, this is only a part of the message that will attract informal entrepreneurs to programs. The other part has to do with the products and services on offer. Here too, the interviews suggest some need for changes to attract these individuals.

Products and Services

Business Development Services

Among the informal entrepreneurs are some candidates for the services that programs currently offer. At the same time, however, there are many for whom the current products don't seem to make sense. One of the biggest challenges that programs face is the reluctance of these entrepreneurs to commit to anything that is perceived as time-intensive. This may be why respondents are reluctant to join a

[54]In 2003, the Nebraska Microenterprise Partnership Fund helped launch a Microenterprise Information Referral System (MIRS), intended to increase referrals of potential clients to microenterprise programs. Under MIRS, program staff meet with bankers and other community leaders, orient them to their program and that of others, and encourage them to make referrals of candidates to programs that don't qualify for bank services. The programs provide technical assistance and financing as indicated and maintain contact with the referring organization for potential future services.

[55]The informal entrepreneurs are not the only ones who need to be convinced of the important role their economic activities play in their communities. In early recruitment drives for REAP, staff would attempt to identify the names and number of entrepreneurs in a community with local officials. Often, these initial efforts would only recognize a small portion of those engaged in business activities. As Rose Jaspersen notes: "In the first community of 400 people, they were proud to show me their list of about 75 businesses that they had identified previously. After we finished our task, they had a list of 189. They were shocked to see how many informal businesses (we didn't use that term) there were and that they had done nothing to help those businesses." E-mail communication, 26 January 2004.

multi-part training or participate in an ongoing peer group.[56] While these in-depth services might make the most sense for moving an entrepreneur from an entry-level enterprise to a more substantial activity, there are too many individuals who are not certain that investing more in their enterprise will make economic or personal sense. For them, more appropriate starter products could include:

- *Feasibility assessment* via training or technical assistance that can focus on the pros and cons of growing the business, and of taking it formal: Will the additional costs incurred in full tax and regulatory compliance bring benefit to the household or not? If yes, then the assistance can move to "risk mitigation" planning — how can the transition be made in a way that protects the household's position while the growth strategy is launched.
- *Assistance with formalization:* step-by-step descriptions of the processes for incorporation and for obtaining licenses and permits for special types of businesses. This can also include explanations of, and assistance with, meeting guidelines for certain product lines, like specialty foods, as well.

Helping Specialty Foods Producers Make the Transition to Formality

Grow Nebraska works with specialty food producers seeking to broaden their markets. For individual entrepreneurs to do this means producing in a commercial kitchen, meeting special labeling requirements, and other regulations. Entrepreneurs are first referred to the University of Nebraska/Lincoln's Food Processing Center for a day-long seminar that walks producers through all aspects of running a food business and the processing required for specific markets. Entrepreneurs are strongly encouraged to develop outsourcing arrangements for production. Grow advises others who are not ready for this step to find a certified kitchen in their local community (often in schools or community centers) that might be available for use, and to go to the state health department for food inspections and certifications. But, these steps can be daunting, as the informal entrepreneurs in this study expressed. Grow Nebraska has found, however, that entrepreneurs who network with others through Grow, and learn of resources available to them, are more inclined to take the next steps. To that end, the organization seeks to develop a mentoring program among foods producers "so that members who have a lot of experience with packaging, outsourcing, shipping, etc., can help the smaller ones learn from their mistakes."* Because mentoring has worked well among their crafters, staff believes that it has great promise for food producers as well.

*E-mail correspondence from Joan Hanson, Grow Nebraska, 19 December 2003.

---

[56]REAP, the Rural Enterprise Assistance Program of the Center for Rural Affairs, supports the formation of peer groups and has a peer group loan product for its clients. Over the last few years, the organization has added an individual loan product, finding that some potential clients were resistant to participating in an ongoing peer process. REAP made this change with some reluctance, believing in the value of peer learning and support, but bowed to the messages it had received through its market research. Its direct lending product has propelled the organization's growth over the last two to three years. For more, see Elaine L. Edgcomb and others, "Organizational Change for Rural Statewide Coverage," *Scaling up Microenterprise Services* (Washington, D.C.: The Aspen Institute/FIELD, May 2002).

Short courses designed to meet the informal entrepreneur where they are — without respect to their formal status — might also be attractive. As with the Latino study, this research uncovered issues around *pricing* — both how to price products and services in relation to their costs, and also how to set prices that the market will accept. While many of the entrepreneurs in this study indicated that they knew they were underpricing themselves, they didn't know by how much or what to do about it. Helping these informal economy entrepreneurs think through this issue would be extremely valuable.

Equally valuable might be helping entrepreneurs understand *ways to decrease their costs.* The difference in cost analyses between two breadmakers in this sample was striking. While one had learned to take every advantage of sales-based purchases and other economizing measures, the other had not. Increasing return has as much to do with cost containment as with better pricing, and the more that entrepreneurs know how to do this, the better.

Programs might also consider whether there are ways to assist small producers through *cooperative buying arrangements.* This might be program-driven, but it might also be producer-driven. Clusters of bakers, quilters or other crafters might be able to drive down the cost of their inputs through their own joint-purchasing efforts.

A third area of interest to these microentrepreneurs was *marketing.* Most marketing was word of mouth directed to family and friends. A few had made business cards and run small ads at different seasons. Most hesitated to do more than that given their informal status. Informal entrepreneurs know that they walk a fine line between needing to be both visible and invisible. Short seminars focused on marketing may help entrepreneurs see how formalization can help them increase their marketing efforts and expand their customer base. There may be special interest in learning about simple ways to increase business through Web marketing. During the course of this study, researchers encountered among the low-income respondents, one individual who had just begun to do some comparative product pricing through an Internet search, and another individual planning to launch her own Web site. In addition, there was at least one moderate-income entrepreneur considering a Web site, but who had taken limited steps to do so. What these entrepreneurs could benefit from is guidance on the whole range of e-commerce strategies available to them — from simple market research to e-mail communication with current customers to market testing on eBay to developing a full-fledged Web site.[57]

While short courses might be one delivery vehicle for reaching these potential clients, other options should be considered. Two other potential vehicles are:

- *Extension service-style technical assistance and*
- *Distance learning.*

These two approaches are at opposite ends of the spectrum. The first is in-person and one-to-one. Based on an agricultural extension agent model, it would offer entrepreneurial assistance wherever and whenever needed, and serve as the

[57]For more on best practices associated with e-commerce, see Karen Doyle, Erika Malm, and others, *Business First: Using Technology to Advance Microenterprise Development,* Best Practice Guide, Volume 5. (Washington, D.C.: The Aspen Institute/FIELD, August 2003). The Guide suggests that entrepreneurs have a variety of e-commerce strategies available to them, and that they should test simpler methods before moving to more complex ones.

link to more in-depth and longer term assistance from other sources. The enterprise agent can serve as the frontline worker both promoting and encouraging the vision of entrepreneurship, as well as offering some immediate technical support. The agent might serve as the entry point to a range of credit and business development services, as well as participate more broadly in the economic development agenda of a set of communities. There is some precedent for this model, which can be implemented part time or full time, but these models are program-based. While informally these program agents make referrals to other programs' services and promote joint ventures, it is not a primary component of their job description. The question is: Can programs band together to finance agents who can more seamlessly and efficiently link entrepreneurs to the services they need, as well as engage more strongly in community-based enterprise promotion? Would additional cross-training of those that are already there help?[58]

Enterprise Agents

The Institute for Social and Economic Development in Iowa expanded its reach in rural areas through a cadre of business development consultants who provided group and one-on-one training and technical assistance to individuals in counties where the demand was insufficient to host a permanent office and staff. The consultants served as the vehicle to both promote and provide services, and costs are kept low by remunerating the agents as contractors for services rendered rather than as staff.

The EDGE program contracts with a local agent to promote its courses in rural Nebraska. The agent has the responsibility to market the program, detect the potential for new training opportunities, and arrange for services to be delivered. The agent is deeply involved in the promotion of entrepreneurship in the regions served, as well as in connecting people to the training program and other resources.

REAP has business specialists assigned to distinct regions of Nebraska offering technical assistance, training and loan products. The specialists are staffed by a small central administrative staff, but operate largely on their own in their regions of interest. REAP has found that there is a direct relationship between the number of specialists in the field and the volume of clients served and loans made.

Distance learning, on the other hand, would offer informal and formal entrepreneurs access to a range of information resources whenever they wanted them. No respondent in this study was aware of any Web sites that could offer them technical information and access to other resources. Even though

[58]As indicated above, the Nebraska rural-focused microenterprise programs have already demonstrated effectiveness with the limited staff that they have. Financing remains a constraint that can't be overlooked. Interestingly, there are some discussions underway in Nebraska regarding community-financed enterprise agents based on a model created by Ernesto Sirolli. The intent is to support growth-potential businesses. Growing the microenterprise organizations' field staff might be a quicker and more cost-effective method of achieving the same end.

microenterprise programs in Nebraska do maintain Web sites that offer information regarding their current products and services, and the University of Nebraska at Lincoln has begun to offer some single topic trainings via the Internet, developing effective courses of this type is not easy. The innovators here have found that it takes a considerable investment in content development, as well as in designing the right type of platform and selecting instructors. Some have also found that the courses are most effective when on-line training is complemented by the opportunities to meet in person.[59] Although expensive to create, this type of venture could make real sense for reaching these informal entrepreneurs, many of whom report Internet access of some type.

Again, creating the service is not enough if entrepreneurs do not know it is there. There are already some Web sites that entrepreneurs could access for answers to questions and referrals, but they appear not to be known by these respondents.[60] Attention to marketing the sites, just like marketing program services, is essential.

Market Development

It is impossible to consider strategies to support rural entrepreneurs without contemplating how programs could further support market development. Increasing access to markets has been one of the most challenging areas for program services in the microenterprise industry, and the learning curve has been steep. Sometimes the response has focused on the establishment of Web malls to display and sell client products, and while they have helped publicize producers' work, they have had less economic pay-off than hoped.[61]

During the course of this study, some small-town efforts to encourage tourism were discovered as well as some notable missed opportunities. A high-end golf course drawing golfers from across the United States, for example, contains a clothing and gift shop that displayed only one local leatherworker's products, those of Robin, who had created a special logo pillow for the course. Certainly there were other crafters who could produce products of a sufficiently high quality to attract the interest of these potential customers.

Grow Nebraska has already demonstrated how a membership organization can increase marketing opportunities for individual crafters and food producers through product placement in organization-operated retail sites, through positioning at larger trade shows and through some Web marketing. Each of these initiatives supports the entrepreneur as an individual business owner, but increases the range of markets she can reach through Grow's connections. What other opportunities

---

[59]For more on best practices associated with distance learning, see Grossman, Malm and others.

[60]There are a range of passive sites and some interactive services available to microentrepreneurs anywhere in the United States. Among others, Count Me In offers a four-session, on-line class at no charge to individuals who are planning to start a business or who have started one in the last six months. The organization also offers one-time technical assistance to entrepreneurs who e-mail a business-related question. The U.S. Small Business Administration's E-Business Institute offers an extensive array of educational resources, including self-directed on-line courses. For more on available resources, see the publication referenced above.

[61]Access to Market strategies operate along the continuum from the supply side (building the capacity of microentrepreneurs to satisfy the market) to the demand side (creating transactions through direct sales), and in between (creating venues for sales and engaging in consumer education through "buy local" campaigns and others). For more on these and lessons learned in program implementation, see Karen Doyle Grossman and others, *Connectors and Conduits: Reaching Competitive Markets from the Ground Up* (Washington, D.C., The Aspen Institute/FIELD, July 2002).

might be created through combining the forces of local community organizations and microenterprise development practitioners? Also, how might "buy local" campaigns increase the local market?

As greater opportunities to reach the market are created, more informal entrepreneurs will be motivated to participate in these services.

Access to Capital

As the previous chapter indicated, only a limited number of these informal entrepreneurs were interested in considering a loan to expand their businesses. A few had already borrowed capital from their local banks, and others were just not certain that they needed to accelerate the growth of their businesses faster than their own accumulation of capital could support. It seems that for most of these entrepreneurs, the first question that needs to be resolved is whether there is indeed a larger market to be tapped, and assuming the potential is there, whether they are willing to take the risk of "going for it." This is why feasibility assessment and the other market development services discussed previously appear to be the more attractive starting points for a relationship with these informal rural entrepreneurs.

Program Policies

If programs are to provide any or all of these services to informal entrepreneurs, they need to clarify their orientation to these potential clients and then make explicit any eligibility criteria for access. Most practitioner programs are adept at helping clients work through the formal logic of a business plan, and most expect that clients who enter with an informal operation are willing to take the next steps toward formalization. In Nebraska, as indicated above, there are several rural microenterprise programs that have thought explicitly about their approach to informal entrepreneurs in this light, and have crafted a set of interactions with potential clients of this type to gauge their interest in moving toward formality, and in taking the next steps to develop their businesses. But, how comfortable are programs in working with informals just as they are? To what extent are they willing to offer services to individuals interested in improving their current operations while staying in the informal economy for the foreseeable future? To what extent are the financial supporters of microenterprise programs understanding of their using resources to support a constituency like this? To what extent are both willing to take the long view?

The industry currently includes programs that have taken both sides of the position. Some will not reject anyone, either because of immigration status or formal business status, and use special funding streams to serve these individuals. Others refuse to work with aspiring entrepreneurs unless they indicate a willingness to become fully licensed, seeing the creation of tax-paying businesses as the right and proper thing to do. Still others occupy a middle ground, offering a limited menu of services to unregistered businesses and using others as a carrot to entice them to formalization.

For program staff, the correct approach is not easy to determine. Just how beneficial is it to Julie, the seamstress, Marilyn, the quilter, and Judith, the bookkeeper, to formalize? On the other hand, shouldn't programs be more wary in working with someone like Tara, with a pre-school in her home, or Paul, the caterer? What about the specialty food producers? Should the health and safety issues in cases like these suggest that programs apply more stringent or progressively stringent requirements for access to services?

The point is that programs need to think through the policies and procedures for working with these clients, and develop a set of guidelines that are clear to staff, that can guide program marketing, and can be made explicit to prospective clients. While it is important to recognize the value of informal entrepreneurship and welcome those engaged in it, the aim should be to have a coherent strategy in doing so that works well for the clients and for the communities in which they work.

Conclusion

More than anything, one comes away from meeting these informal, rural entrepreneurs impressed — impressed by their willingness to work hard, by their commitment to their families and communities, and by their general acceptance of the rules of the game. These are individuals who generally pay taxes and abide by the larger economic regulations that affect their lives, but who find themselves operating on the margins in small ways in order to make ends meet. They are far from scofflaws who flout the rules.

These are also individuals who demonstrate just how hard it is to live the American dream today. Unlike the Latino and African-American informal entrepreneurs discussed in the earlier monographs in this series, these are individuals who, on the surface, have more going for themselves, at least in terms of having greater assets to their names. They are small land holders and homeowners, but they are in a region where such assets may be depreciating and their liquidity in ever sharper decline. Despite their assets, they face a yearly struggle to make ends meet, to gain more than they spend on cattle ranching, and to hold onto the various jobs that make up their economic portfolio. They live in a region where their children's economic fortunes may require them to go far afield from the communities in which they were raised, and which their parents hold in high esteem.

Can these individuals be helped by microenterprise services? Do their small-scale economic activities hold any promise for growth and greater return? Or is it better to "let well enough alone," not complicating their efforts through formalizaton? Certainly this study would suggest that at least part of this population, possibly a third or so, would be candidates at any given time. This group contains those who express ambition and interest in growth, as well as those who would cautiously consider it. Both would benefit from the type of sound business analysis and guidance that is embedded in high-quality microenterprise programs, especially if these services could be adapted to the specific needs, and time and place constraints of these busy entrepreneurs.

This study also suggests that microenterprise programs in rural areas have important roles to play in addition to offering direct services to individuals. They include helping local communities to truly see, appreciate and support the entrepreneurs in their midst, as well as helping informal economy entrepreneurs look at their own work afresh, and understand it from a business perspective. They also include working at policy levels to help interested policymakers and government officials build and fully fund structures and incentives that will enhance what is already there for those with eyes to see. Many of the needed tools and strategies needed are known. What's required now is to expand and deepen these efforts for the benefit of many more.

Appendix A: Research Methodology

FIELD designed and implemented this qualitative research study with a view to collecting detailed and rich information regarding the informal microenterprise activities of rural microentrepreneurs in the United States. It was hoped that this work would enhance the literature available on the informal economy in this country by providing a more complete picture of the intersection between microenterprise and the informal economy, an area not fully explored in other literature.

Research Questions

As mentioned in the Introduction, the research questions established for this study included the following:

1. What is the nature of informal economic activities within rural communities?
2. Why do people participate in the informal economy? What incentives exist for informal economic activities and what barriers hinder participation in the mainstream economy?
3. What are the survival strategies of rural residents who participate in the informal economy? How are informal economic activities patched together, with each other and with more traditional income streams, to support individuals and their families?
4. How do informal microentrepreneurs not participating in microenterprise development programs differ from those who have approached programs for services? Are there differences in business size or the revenues generated?
5. What are the opportunities for and barriers to growth for informal enterprises?
6. What are the implications for microenterprise development programs?

Research Locations

The specific counties visited will not be identified in this report. A number of respondents were concerned that their identities could be determined just through a description of their occupations and county location. However, they reside in seven of the 51 counties described as "rural farm" counties, counties with an agriculturally-based economy (20 percent or more of county income from agriculture) and with no population center of 2,500 or more.[62]

[62]Jon M. Bailey and Kim Preston, "Swept Away: Chronic Hardship and Fresh Promise on the Rural Great Plains. A Socio-Economic Study of the Rural Great Plains," Center for Rural Affairs: June 2003.

Research Design

FIELD staff implemented a qualitative research design in these settings. The design had three elements: a purposive sampling method, an open-ended semi-structured interview process and content analysis of the data collected.

Sampling Methodology

FIELD used a purposive sampling methodology aimed at maximum variation in terms of the cases selected. Respondents selected for interviewing met a set of criteria. They needed to be:

- Adults between 20 and 65 years old;
- Low-income;
- Inclusive of both men and women;
- Currently operating an informal business or having done so in the last 12 months;
- Not associated with any microenterprise program, nor received assistance for their businesses from any source;
- Representative of a broad array of microenterprise types.

Excluded from the study were individuals who did not have a consistent history of working informally, or who did not work "on their own account," but solely in a continuing employer-employee relationship.

The interviewers recruited potential respondents through a local consultant home-based in the target region and with extensive contacts in the communities. The consultant arranged local press coverage of the study and announced that interviews were being conducted in western Nebraska. The articles included contact information for individuals interested in participating. Although the study was publicized, the overwhelming majority of interviews were conducted with individuals identified through the consultant's contacts in the community.

All potential respondents were screened by telephone to verify that the person met the study criteria. Interviews were scheduled at a variety of public buildings in the seven counties: courthouses, a library and a church. In one community the interviews were conducted in rented space as public facilities were not available.

The Interview

Two interviewers conducted all the interviews. Occasionally, both interviewers conducted the interviews together, but generally, interviews were scheduled concurrently with each interviewer conducting a separate interview. Interviewers were FIELD staff persons experienced in qualitative research and expert in microenterprise development. Interviews were conducted in English in all cases.

The interviews were based upon a guide that contained a set of open-ended questions that allowed the interviewers and respondents to explore a wide range of issues together. The interview covered the respondent's history of engagement in the informal economy — how the individual became involved in his/her particular enterprise, how many hours does s/he engage in it, who the customers are and how are they found, what s/he earns from the enterprise, and what is invested in it.

If the individual had multiple informal enterprises, all were discussed, as was the respondent's current employment experience if s/he was also employed. Respondents were also asked to discuss their motivations for having an informal enterprise, their perceptions regarding the positive and negative aspects of working this way, and what their goals were with respect to this work. If the respondent was interested in growing the enterprise, s/he was also asked what she might need to help its development. Respondents were also asked about their household situation and whether other household members worked informally as well, and whether they knew others who had informal enterprises. While the interviews generally followed the flow of the guide, the interviewers adapted the wording and sequence of the questions, and added others, to conform to the stories told by specific respondents in the context of the actual interview. The interview concluded with some closed-ended questions regarding age, educational level, marital status and household income.

The interviews were conducted between September and October 2003. Each lasted between 45 minutes and 90 minutes. All interviews were tape-recorded and 29 were completed. Each respondent was provided $75 in payment for his/her time and willingness to share his/her experiences with the interviewers. Respondents were promised confidentiality with respect to the use of their names and other identifying information.

Analysis

All interviews were transcribed and subjected to a content analysis that involved a search for overall patterns and themes with response to the key questions asked. In addition, the interviews of ranching households and townspeople were studied separately with the intent of understanding and describing their different experiences. Distinctions were also made between informal work and self-employment or microenterprise. Within self-employment or microenterprise, individual sectors and growth potential businesses were further organized and analyzed as it became clear that markets and motivations were distinguishing characteristics of the entrepreneurs interviewed. Some additional secondary research accompanied the analysis of issues expressed by rural farm county inhabitants. In particular, this involved seeking additional information with respect to the New Homestead Act, cattle prices, existent microenterprise support programs and so forth. This secondary research enabled the interviewers to better understand the context in which the interview subjects worked informally and operated their businesses, as well as their prospects for future growth and assistance of a wide variety.

Interview Guide

Name of Interviewee: ______________________________

Telephone Number: ______________________________

Referral Organization/Person: ______________________________

Date of Interview: ________________ Length of Interview: __________

Introduction: The purpose of this interview is to help us better understand the reasons people work informally — I'm referring here to any jobs that you don't pay taxes on — jobs you are paid in cash or you may exchange services to receive something other than cash in return. Sometimes this is referred to as working off-the-books, under-the-table, or moonlighting.

I'd like to ask you some questions about your experiences working informally to learn more about this type of work. I'm not a tax person or connected with the IRS in any way. I won't report anything we discuss with the IRS. My only purpose is to learn from your experiences.

Before we begin, I would like you to know everything you share with me today will be kept absolutely confidential. We're interviewing 50 people so your experiences will be combined with the answers others have given. No names will be used in the report.

RESPONDENT'S SITUATION

1. What is your current work situation? [This is just a checklist to keep interview organized. Everyone will be either currently working in the informal economy or has worked in the informal economy within the past 12 months. But, not everyone will also have wage employment.]

___ Currently working in the informal economy

___ Not currently working in the informal economy, but has in the last 12 months

___ Also works at regular, wage employment

Respondent's Primary Informal Work

Now, let's talk more about the details of your informal work. I'd like to learn as much as I can about your work. (NOTE: If person does more than one type of informal work, ask person to talk first about the informal work that s/he considers to be the primary one, and indicate you'll ask questions about the other work later.)

2. What sort of informal work do/did you do?

3. How did you first start out working informally in this line of work?

4. How long have you done this particular work?

5. In a typical week, how many hours do/did you work informally?

6. Do/Did you work for yourself or do you work through someone else?

   6a. IF SELF-EMPLOYED ASK:

   - Who are/were your primary customers or clients?

   - How do/did you find out about future jobs?

   - Do/did you advertise, is it by word-of-mouth, or do people approach you?

   6b. IF WORKS FOR SOMEONE ELSE ASK:

   - Do/Did you work for a company? If yes, how many other people work in the type of arrangement that you do? Are there some people who are employees and earn a wage rather than working informally?

   - How did you learn about this opportunity — did someone approach you or did you approach your employer?

7. How are/were you paid?

   PROBE: Are/Were you paid in cash, by check, or through some other arrangement?

8. Do/Did you receive any benefits through your informal work, such as use of equipment, reduction on uniform costs, health insurance, sick days or vacation days?

9. Is/Was this the first informal work that you have done?

Benefits and Motivations of Informal Work

10. What aspects about working informally do you like best? What are the greatest benefits?

11. What aspects about working informally do you like least? What are the biggest problems?

12. What led you to seek informal work? How did you first get started working this way?

13. Do you imagine yourself earning income through informal work in the future?

14. What would need to happen for you to stop working in the informal economy and either go into business for yourself or have full-time wage employment?

Respondent's Other Informal Work

NOTE: IF PERSON HAS/HAD MORE THAN ONE INFORMAL JOB, ASK:

15. We've just talked about your primary informal work and you mentioned earlier that you do/did more than one type of informal work, tell me about your other informal work.

16. How many hours in a typical week do you work for this other informal job? PROBE: So in addition to the hours you work at the informal work we discussed earlier, you work ...

17. How much do you earn in a typical week from this other informal work?

Respondent's Wage Employment

IF ALSO WORKING FORMAL WAGE EMPLOYMENT ASK:

18. Other than your informal work, you also mentioned you have wage employment — by this I mean a job that you pay taxes on. What do you do for regular wage employment?

19. In a typical week, how many hours do you work for wage employment? PROBE: So in addition to the hours you work at the informal work we discussed earlier, you work ...

20. How much do you earn in a typical week from wage employment?

Interviewer's Summary

21. You've told me a lot of detailed information and I would like to make certain I have a clear picture of what you do. So, before we move on to some different questions, let me just summarize what I've learned so far. From your primary informal work, you work an average of ___ hours each week and earn roughly _____ each week. From your other informal work, you ... From your wage employment, you ...

(NOTE: TABLE BELOW IS TO HELP INTERVIEWER JOT DOWN SUMMARY DETAILS AND PROBE IF THERE IS ANY NEW INFORMATION SHARED AT THIS TIME.)

	Average hours per week	**Average earnings per week**
Primary informal work		
Other informal work		
Wage employment		

OTHER HOUSEHOLD MEMBERS

22. We've talked a lot about your experiences, now I'd like to ask you some questions about other members of your household. I'd like to get a picture of any informal work they might do.

    22a. How many people are there in your household? __________

    22b. In the last 12 months, did other members of your household earn cash to make ends meet in ways other than regular wage employment?

    22c. Has this been the case for a long time or is this something new, temporary, seasonal?

    22d. If so, what type of work? Please describe. How many hours do they work? How much do they earn per week? NOTE: May wish to fill-in table below to keep numbers straight.

Family member (name not needed — refer by relationship to respondent)	**Describe informal work**	**Average hours per week**	**Average earnings per week**

FRIENDS/NEIGHBORS

23. We would like to understand how widespread working informally is — do you have friends, co-workers or neighbors who are also working informally? Is it fairly typical for people you know to work informally or is this rare? Could you tell me a little about the type of work they are doing?

WRAP-UP

24. Is there anything else about informal work that I need to know to really understand what informal work is and why it is so popular?

DEMOGRAPHIC ITEMS

Before we end, I just have a few personal questions to ask you. These questions help us get a picture of who works informally. Again, everything you share will be kept confidential.

D1. What race or ethnic group do you consider yourself? CIRCLE ONLY ONE

AFRICAN AMERICAN

WHITE

LATINA OR HISPANIC

ASIAN OR PACIFIC ISLANDER

NATIVE AMERICAN (AMERICAN INDIAN)

MULTI-RACIAL

OTHER? (SPECIFY)______________________________

D2. Gender: FEMALE MALE

D3. What is your current marital status? CIRCLE ONLY ONE

MARRIED

SEPARATED

DIVORCED

WIDOWED

NEVER BEEN MARRIED, SINGLE

LIVE-IN SITUATION

D4. How much education have you had? CIRCLE ONLY ONE

LESS THAN HIGH SCHOOL (Indicate highest grade completed ________)

COMPLETED HIGH SCHOOL OR EARNED GED

SOME COLLEGE

2-YEAR COLLEGE DEGREE

4-YEAR COLLEGE DEGREE

ATTENDED GRADUATE SCHOOL

GRADUATE DEGREE

OTHER: ______________________________________

Thank you very much for your time. I really enjoyed learning about your experiences.

References

ACCION USA. *Executive Summary: The Microlending Market in the U.S.,* October 1999.

"Amid Dying Plains Towns, One Makes a Last Stand for New Jobs and People." *New York Times,* 1 December 2003, A:1, 18.

Bailey, Jon M. and Kim Preston. *Swept Away: Chronic Hardship and Fresh Promise on the Rural Great Plains: A Socio-Economic Study of the Rural Great Plains.* Walthill, Nebraska: Center for Rural Affairs, June 2003.

"Bison Burgers, for Humanity's Sake." *New York Times,* 5 October 2003, 3:1.

Castells, Manuel and Alejandro Portes. "World Underneath: The Origins, Dynamics, and Effects of the Informal Economy." In *The Informal Economy: Studies in Advanced and Less Developed Countries,* eds. Alejandro Portes, Manuel Castells and Lauren A. Benton. Baltimore: Johns Hopkins Press, 1989.

Chen, Martha and Elizabeth Dunn. *Household Economic Portfolios.* Washington, D.C.: U.S. Agency for International Development, AIMS, 1996; available from http://www.usaidmicro.org/pubs/pubsTemplate.asp?page=/componen/aims/pubs/english/desk7.htm; Internet.

Clark, Peggy and Amy Kays. *Microenterprise and the Poor.* Washington, D.C.: The Aspen Institute, 1999.

Doyle Grossman, Karen, Tamra Thetford, and Amy Kays Blair. *Connectors and Conduits: Reaching Competitive Markets from the Ground Up.* Washington, D.C.: The Aspen Institute/FIELD, July 2002.

Doyle Grossman, Karen, Erika Malm, Veronica Francis, and Candace Nelson. *Business First: Using Technology to Advance Microenterprise Development,* Best Practice Guide, Volume 5. Washington, D.C.: The Aspen Institute/FIELD, August 2003.

Dunn, Barry H. "Measuring Cow-Calf Profitability and Financial Efficiency." South Dakota State University: unpublished manuscript, 2003.

Edgcomb, Elaine and Maria Medrano Armington. *The Informal Economy: Latino Enterprises at the Margins.* Washington, D.C.: The Aspen Institute/FIELD, 2003.

Ehrenreich, Barbara. *Nickel and Dimed: On (Not) Getting By in America.* New York: Henry Holt and Company, 2001.

Losby, Jan L., Marcia E. Kingslow and John F. Else. *The Informal Economy: Experiences of African Americans.* Washington, D.C.: The Aspen Institute, 2003.

Losby, Jan L., Marcia E. Kingslow, John F. Else, Elaine L. Edgcomb, Erika T. Malm and Vivian Kao. *Informal Economy Literature Review.* Washington, D.C.: The Aspen Institute/FIELD, December 2002; available from http://www.fieldus.org/li/pdf/InformalEconomy.pdf; Internet.

"Making Way for Buffalo." *New York Times,* 29 October 2003, A: 25.

Malm, Erika. "The Informal Economy and Microenterprise in the United States." *FIELD forum* Issue 14. Washington, D.C.: The Aspen Institute/FIELD, March 2003; available from http://www.fieldus.org/publications/Field_Forum14.pdf; Internet.

NGA Center for Best Practices. "Innovative State Policy Options to Promote Rural Economic Development." NGA Center for Best Practices, Issue Brief, Economic and Technology Policy Studies, February 2003.

Popper, Frank and Deborah. *The Buffalo Commons as Regional Metaphor and Geographic Method.* Available from http://www.gprc.org/buffalo_commons_popper.html; Internet.

Portes, Alejandro, Manuel Castells and Lauren A. Benton. "Conclusion: the Policy Implications of Informality." In *The Informal Economy: Studies in Advanced and Less Developed Countries,* eds. Alejandro Portes, Manuel Castells and Lauren A. Benton, 306-307. Baltimore: Johns Hopkins University Press, 1989.

Reding, Nick. "Story of a Steak." *Food and Wine,* November 2003. Available from http://www.foodandwine.com/invoke.cfm?objectid=EFA8B641-6A00-4436-89A78195CDDF80F0; Internet.

Rural Enterprise Assistance Project/Center for Rural Affairs. "Organizational Change for Rural Statewide Coverage." *Scaling up Microenterprise Services,* ed. Elaine L. Edgcomb, 81-99. Washington, D.C.: The Aspen Institute/FIELD, May 2002.

"U.S. Mad Cow case to cut 2004 cattle prices — USDA." *Forbes.com.* Reuters report to Forbes.com, 12 January 2004, 8:52AM ET. Available from http://www.forbes.com/home_europe/newswire/2004/01/12/rtr1206844.html; Internet.

U.S. Department of Agriculture. "National Weekly Cattle and Beef Summary." USDA Livestock and Grain Market News. Newsletter on-line, 27 October 2003; available from http://www.ams.usda.gov/mnreports/lm_ct150.txt; Internet.

U.S. Department of Commerce Bureau of Economic Analysis. "National Income and Product Account Tables." Tables on-line, 8 July 2003; available from http://www.bea.doc.gov/bea/dn/nipaweb/TableViewFixed.asp?SelectedTable=17&FirstYear=2002&LastYear=2003&Freq=Qtr; Internet.

Walker, Britton A. and Amy Kays Blair. *2002 Directory of U.S. Microenterprise Programs.* Washington, D.C.: The Aspen Institute/FIELD, 2002.